EDINBURGH
EDUCATION AND SOCIETY
SERIES

General Editor: Colin Bell

Trying Work

Gender, Youth and Work Experience

Anne Stafford

EDINBURGH UNIVERSITY PRESS

© Anne Stafford 1991
22 George Square, Edinburgh

Distributed in North America
by Columbia University Press
New York

Set in Linotron Palatino
by Koinonia Ltd, Bury, and
printed in Great Britain by
Page Bros Ltd, Norwich

British Library Cataloguing
    in Publication Data
Stafford, Anne
    Trying work: gender, youth and
    work experience.
    I. Great Britain. Young persons.
    Work experience.
    1. Title
    331.342592941

ISBN 0 7486 0205 4 (cased)

CONTENTS

ACKNOWLEDGEMENTS

I want to begin with a word to all the people whose help, time and co-operation made this book possible: first of all to the supervisors and staff in the workshop. The whole argument of this study suggests that the root of why teenagers' lives were the way they were (and still are to a great extent) lies in changes in the economy, and in the way our society is organised. These would have to change for any very fundamental alterations in teenagers' lives to take place. But, as it stands, this offers little consolation for supervisors and administrators who, every day, are confronted with managing such schemes as those I describe.

My time in Seafield left me with absolutely no doubt that the group of people working there were highly motivated and deeply caring. They undoubtedly had the very best interests of the trainees at heart. And if at times this study makes them seem harsh, or sometimes portrays them as failing, this has little to do with them as individuals and everything to do with the fact that they were faced with a difficult job. It was the task that was impossible. In a society which could not offer jobs to its school leavers these workers were on the front line, trying to make sense of youth unemployment and of the Government's half measures to cope with it.

I am also deeply indebted to the trainees for accepting me and finding me space to try to understand their lives. In the book I reveal many private details, the highs and lows of their daily existence, their secrets, fantasies: events which portray them at their most courageous, at their most vulnerable. I feel grateful, if ambiguous, that I was able to do it, and have done everything possible to try to protect their anonymity, for example by changing names and venue. But some violation of privacy remains. If this is justified, it is in the belief that at a time when there was mass youth unemployment, when the very basis of what it meant to be young and leaving school was beginning to be redefined, the implication of these changes should not remain hidden and unacknowledged.

I would like to thank Ian Day and Adrian Sinfield for their academic support throughout the thesis.

I am particularly grateful to my mother and father and I dedicate this book to them. Thanks to all of my relatives for their unqualified support (financial and emotional) – to Val, Carol, Pauline, Joe, Mary, Josie, Cathy, Joe and to John. Thanks also to my friends for their support and encouragement. Unlike the young people in my study, I could find the experience of unemployment tolerable – my friends kept me solvent.

INTRODUCTION

In the four years from 1978 hundreds of thousands of young, working-class Scots had their first taste of working life courtesy of the Manpower Services Commission's (MSC) Youth Opportunities Programme (YOP). The process was continued and expanded into the 1980s with the Youth Training Scheme (YTS). Through both of these schemes the process of young people's entry to the labour market was fundamentally and radically changed.

While much has been written about the impact of YOP and YTS on the apprenticeship system, education and industry, there has been almost no attention paid to understanding and detailing the effect of such major changes on the lives of young people themselves. This book is an attempt to put this right. It is first and foremost a book about working-class teenagers in Scotland. It consists of five months' participant observation of young people taking part in an MSC training workshop. It took place in 1981/2, two years into Mrs Thatcher's government and several years into the deepest recession for half a century which brought levels of unemployment unprecedented in the post-war period. My aim was to document the lives of these young people, to look at how they made their relationships to each other and to the workshop.

Firstly I would like to look at what other people have written about young people, their culture, the MSC and the nature of its involvement in their lives.

YOUTH CULTURE

My interest in youth culture originated in the work of the Centre for Contemporary Cultural Studies (CCCS) in Birmingham. Work produced there in the 1970s had direct links back to classic American deviancy studies of the 1950s. Books like W. F. Whyte's *Street Corner Society* (1955) and Albert Cohen's *Delinquent Boys* (1955) were part of this tradition. Studies like these looked at the lives and the detailed culture of working-class boys. Based on a methodology of participant observation, they marked at the time a break with mainstream sociology. The Birmingham studies in the 1970s continued this tradition, looking at everything from Teds to Mods to Skin Heads and so on.[1] They were an attempt to understand the conditions under which young people were disruptive. Themes of rebelliousness and resistance to authority were central to the Birmingham Centre's work.

One of the problems with such studies was that they focused on a particular section of young people and left out consideration of any others. One comment was that: 'They have typically concentrated on unconventional fractions of youth – especially working class youth, the fascination for the bizarre, the esoteric, the pathological, the marginal elements of youth behaviour and ideology...' (Mungham 1976). Other studies have, however, tried to understand more ordinary young people and their culture.[2] Another limitation of this literature is that it concentrates almost solely on boys. Attempts to understand the lives and culture of working-class teenage girls have been almost completely absent from this literature.

Frances Heidensohn claims that classic participant observation studies in the 1950s marked the 'start of the long, romantic attachment of sociologists of deviance to delinquents as heroes'. College boys meet corner boys! Another author claims it is no accident that these studies originated in Chicago! (Roberts 1975: 246). He states: '... the participant observer is the man (and the image is characteristically male) who has looked "real life" in the eye, the "guy who's done the leg work"; the person who's seen it all. Perhaps the fact that so much participant observation has been done in Chicago has contributed to this "private eye image".' More recently this criticism has been taken on board and there are now a number of cultural studies of teenage girls. McRobbie (1984), Griffin (1985), Lees (1986), Cockburn (1987) have all put girls centre-stage and have analysed different aspects of their lives and cultures.

The problem with the early literature is not simply that it did a disservice to girls by leaving them out, it has also had implications for our understanding of boys and masculinity. This is perhaps best understood with reference to one book; *Learning to Labour* (1977) by Paul Willis was very significant and provided the framework for my own thinking in relation to young people. If my own work has taught me to be critical of Willis, it is the criticism of someone who has learned a lot from him. Although he writes in the same tradition, Willis does go further than other studies. Unlike others, he sees gender as an important consideration in understanding the culture of teenage boys. The basic question for Willis was why the so called 'lads' in his study were content voluntarily to take on board the definition of themselves as manual labourers (Willis 1977). Through a complex (and not a predictable) process his 'lads' rejected 'mental labour' and came to accept themselves as manual labourers. And in coming to this acceptance (argues Willis), they gleaned radical insights. The important thing about this for Willis was not so much the radical insights themselves, but the fact that these insights were not transformed into political action. It was this that locked them into a lifetime of manual labour. For him, gender was central to this process. Gender and class, working together, brought some sections of working-class youth to a complicated acceptance of themselves as manual labourers. Though this book, like earlier studies, is a book about the more colourful sections of working-class youth, by introducing gender into the analysis Willis added a whole new layer of understanding to the debate.

However, there are aspects of the substance of Willis's analysis with which I cannot agree. In many ways this is not surprising. Although the period in which he did his fieldwork was less than ten years from mine in terms of chronology, it is in fact separated by a chasm. His 'lads' were confident they could find manual jobs – his question was why they embraced them. For their younger brothers who took part in my study in the early 1980s, even these 'dead-end jobs' had moved completely out of reach. Yet I do not think the main difference between my study and Willis is simply this.

Though the concept of gender was important to Willis, he too chose to focus only on boys. That, I would argue, makes his study limited. He cannot of course be blamed for it personally; it is difficult to imagine how a male researcher could achieve the familiarity with girls' worlds that he achieved with boys'. (It is an odd consequence of male power that female researchers – being inconsequential – may find it easier to study males ethnographically.) But men and masculinity are not set constant, they are formed and reformed all the time, in relation to women and femininity. One is the flip side of the other; you cannot, I would argue, fully understand one except in relation to the other.[3] This, I suppose, is a feminist criticism of Willis. But my point is not the normal feminist one that Willis under-estimates the effect of gender; paradoxically, he overestimates it. Specifi-cally, he mistakes for gender, for masculinity, what are in fact phenomena of class. Let me explain: Willis's understanding of boys was as an insider. His ideas about girls were formed wholly on the basis of how girls seemed superficially in relation to boys. When it came to girls Willis saw what boys saw: 'the resolution among working class girls of the contradiction between being sexually desirable but not sexually experienced leads to behaviour which ... takes the form of romanticism readily fed by teenage magazines. What the 'lads' see of the romantic behaviour they have partly conditioned in the girls, however, is simple sheepishness, weakness and a silly indi-rectness in social relationships.' (Willis 1977: 45). And it is true. In relation to boys, girls are like this. But it is only partly true. Willis did not and could not see the rest. The public face of girls as they relate to boys is only the tip of a very hidden iceberg and it is important that analyses of girls are not left at this level. Descriptions like these must be set against more complete accounts of their lives. 'Confused' and 'passive' accounts of girls must be set against the background of what happens in their own autonomous culture, where they can be very different: witty, confident, assured and engaged in a vigorous culture of their own and, as we shall see, in a way that is not too different from the 'lads' in Paul Willis's study.

This book is a participant observation study of working-class teenagers. And it attempts to understand those teenagers who were 'ordinary' as well as those who were not. It is also different in that it is not simply a study of boys, nor is it only a study of girls; it attempts to look at the experiences of both girls and boys. The study is different in one other important aspect. Unlike any other study of teenage culture, it focuses on the lives and culture of young people in Scotland. The study is based on the experiences of the young Scottish people who participated in a local training workshop, part of the then Youth Opportunities Programme (YOP) in the early eighties. I tried to unravel a complicated story and to understand the complex process through which the ideas of the workshop were imposed on these young people and the extent to which they accepted or rejected it. I used participant observation to gauge the everyday way in which their lives were affected and changed, and indeed the way in which their culture was brought to bear on the workshop. I tried to bear in mind that this experience would be different for girls and boys.

Before I begin, however, I need to put the workshop in context by outlining the programme I studied (YOP), its introduction in 1978, the reasons for its introduction and what it was about in practice.

THE MSC, YOUTH UNEMPLOYMENT AND YOUTH TRAINING, 1979 TO 1988

For the reader who has a particular interest in the MSC and its programmes there are a number of texts which address this in detail, for example, Finn (1987) on the MSC's youth provision, Ainley and Corney (1990) on the MSC in general and Brown and Fairley (1990) on the MSC in Scotland, also Raffe (1984a) and Furlong (1988). This outline of the YOP in Scotland draws heavily on Fairley (1990).

The main reason YOP was introduced is complicated. The story began in the late 1970s when unemployment was growing and complacent assumptions about 'full employment in a mixed economy' were beginning to disappear. Unemployment in Scotland doubled in the second half of the 1970s and again in the second half of the 1980s (Fraser and Sinfield (1987), quoted in Brown 1990). Within the general problem of unemployment, youth unemployment was becoming a particular area of concern. It had been rising dramatically from 1974. In July of that year there were 80 000 under-20s unemployed in Britain. Two years later there were 390 000 (Loney 1983: 27). Between 1972 and 1977 the number of unemployed 16 and 17-year-olds rose by 120 per cent (Frith 1980: 25).

The focus on youth

The government, through the mechanism of the MSC, ploughed enormous resources into alleviating the consequences of youth unemployment. Various MSC schemes made a major impact on the lives of hundreds of thousands of young Scots. It may be worth dwelling for a moment on this overriding concern with and focus on young people. David Raffe (1984a: 189) lists some of the reasons why young people's unemployment presented a problem for the government of the day and why public concern about it was at the time running high. The higher unemployment rate among young people compared with adults inspired feelings of compassion and injustice. And since young people were not responsible for Britain's social and economic plight, why should they be made to suffer? Also, young people 'cannot be blamed' for their own unemployment in the same way that older workers are held to be 'losing jobs' with 'excessive pay' demands and 'restrictive practices' (Markall and Gregory 1982: 59).

A number of factors pertaining to young people themselves can also help explain the massive state response to their unemployment. The threat of political and social unrest by idle, bored, young people was undoubtedly a major theme structuring the nature of the provision. Geoff Mungham (1982) argued that this particular concern has long historical roots. From the nineteenth century at least the idea of 'workless youth' and the idea of crime and moral degeneration have gone hand in hand. Examples from literature at the time express sentiments about (male) youth that has a very contemporary ring to it. 'Loose, single men' '... with no commitment to or a stake in the prevailing order' 'in danger of contaminating respectable and industrious youth' (Mungham 1982: 30).

Youth unemployment

The reasons why youth unemployment rose so sharply compared to adult unemployment at this time are also complicated. The report on unemployment from the House of Commons Committee on Scottish Affairs in 1981/2 'identified the factors influencing the level of youth unemployment as demographic change (in the population of young people in the relevant age group); labour market competition (resulting from the increase in female participation rates); and the increase in the wage levels for young people in relation to adult workers, especially in the 1970s.' (Brown 1990: 17).

Some authors argued that youth unemployment was the result of deep structural changes in the economy: that it was those sectors of industry which young people traditionally entered (like manufacturing, distribution and transport) which experienced the greatest job losses (Rees and Atkinson 1982: 3). They claimed that youth unemployment was partly due to changes in the kind of workers employers were demanding and that in a time of increasing supply of labour, employers had no need to employ young workers. Others at the time, for example David Raffe (1985b), argued that youth unemployment was in fact less entrenched, structural and permanent than this. Raffe claimed that there was no evidence that employers were deliberately discriminating against young people (Raffe 1985a: 26). He suggested that youth unemployment was a cyclical phenomenon and largely the result of the recession.

The nature of unemployment in the late 1970s and early 1980s was complicated, uneven and difficult to unravel. And while it is important to try to understand it, it is more important at least for the purposes of this study to try to establish the aims and assumptions which lay behind policymakers' attempts to alleviate it. To do this it is first of all necessary to understand a little bit about the MSC.

The MSC

The MSC began as a small, relatively insignificant planning agency in 1974, becoming a very large government agency in the 1980s. The main reason for its growth was escalating youth unemployment and the numerous schemes introduced to cope with it as recognition of its scale and political importance grew in the late 1970s.

The special programmes

Youth unemployment was understood, at least initially, as short-term and cyclical. Subsidies and inducements to industry, in the form of the Job Creation Scheme[4] and the Work Experience Programme[5] were originally set up for three years. They constituted contingency plans in anticipation of an economic revival (Markall 1982: 82). In the face of escalating youth unemployment and when the so-called temporary measures should have disappeared, the analysis was changing. The Holland Report published in 1977, and out of which YOP emerged, was the first scheme introduced specifically for young people. If not assuming that youth unemployment was deep-seated and permanent, it was at the very least defining it as a 'medium term feature of the economy' (MSC 1978).

> There is some uncertainty among labour market analysts whether the current level of unemployment among young people is 'structural' or 'cyclical'. In the past recessions young people's employment rose more quickly than total employment as the recession set in and fell more quickly in the recovery from recession. It is not clear whether this pattern would still hold, but in the context of the Commission's planning assumptions the issue does not really arise. Since unemployment seems likely to remain high, so too will young people's unemployment. (MSC, 1978a quoted in Markall and Gregory 1982: 65.)

Youth unemployment was now recognised as a long-term problem and a priority in terms of funding. And YOP was set up with the strong multi-partite consensus of bodies such as the CBI, the TUC, the government, local government and education authorities.

In Scotland in 1978/9 there were 23 600 participants on YOP. By 1980/81 the scheme had practically doubled with 49 300. By 1982/3 YOP was catering for more than half of all the school-leavers entering the labour market (Raffe 1988) and it was accounting for more than 40 per cent of the

MSC budget. Over the whole life of the programme between 1978/9 and 1982/3 nearly one quarter of a million young Scots entered the programme (Fairley 1990).

YOP offered work experience to unemployed 16–18-year-olds to enable them to gain experience of working life which would be recognised as valuable by employers. Work Experience on Employers' Premises (WEEP) constituted the bulk of the provision. Trainees were also placed in Training Workshops and did Project-based Work Experience. There was also input (usually in the form of Work Preparation and Life and Social Skills) from Colleges of Further Education. WEEP was the cheapest form of provision with a filled place on WEEP costing less than half of a training workshop place. In Scotland in 1980/81 more than 60 per cent of participants did WEEP, 14 per cent did Work Preparation and training workshops provided about 8 per cent of places. Training workshops were a relatively more important part of MSC provision in Scotland than in Britain as a whole (Fairley 1990). Within YOP, WEEP was seen as the top of an unofficial hierarchy tending to have the best record for placing trainees in jobs afterwards. Project-based WE tended to be seen to be for young people of lower educational attainment.

Initially YOP had a successful record of placing the young people who had been through programmes in work. In the early days of the scheme 80 per cent of young people moved into paid work. As it expanded, however, it did not manage to sustain this kind of success. Its popularity declined as it grew. YOP was criticised as providing low-quality training, for being a source of 'cheap labour' and open to abuse by unscrupulous employers. Young trainees substituting for adult labour was seen to be one of the main problems. The MSC's own monitoring of the scheme and its abuses was widely criticised. In particular job substitution was believed to be high and this seemed to be borne out by the MSC's own research (Fairley 1990).

With the introduction of the Youth Training Scheme (YTS) in 1982/3 the MSC had transformed and widened its objectives. And while YOP had been concerned with providing experience of work for unemployed young people, YTS was supposed to cater ultimately for all early school-leavers and initially concentrated on sixteen-year-olds. YTS was intended to improve on YOP, become a permanent scheme and leave behind the poor image which YOP had amongst young people, parents and others.

The so-called New Training Initiative (NTI) out of which YTS emerged had two main objectives relating to young people:

> To develop skill training and apprenticeship in such a way as to enable young people entering at different educational attainments to acquire agreed standards of skill appropriate to the jobs available and to provide them with a basis for progress through further learning.

> To move towards a position where all young people under the age of 18 have the opportunity either of continuing in full-time education

or of entering a period of planned work experience combined with work-related training and education. (quoted in Fairley 1990: 53.) The plans for Scotland were for 45 to 50 000 sixteen-year-old school-leavers with some 460 000 places for sixteen-year-olds throughout Britain. Young people on YTS took part in either Mode A schemes on employers' premises or in community-based Mode B schemes. These were approximately two Mode A schemes to every Mode B scheme. Mode B schemes were often viewed as a second best to Mode A schemes with employers.

YTS quickly became the largest scheme operated by the MSC. In 1983/4 YTS represented £73·5m out of a total MSC budget of £118·6m. And of 646 staff in Scotland in April 1983, 497 were involved with YTS (Fairley 1990: 55). Despite the attempt to take on board the earlier problems with YOP, the quality of provision under YTS remained similar in the early years. By 1983 it was already clear that the population of school-leavers was set to decline in the second part of the 1980s. To address problems of quality and the declining numbers of young people likely to enter the labour market, the MSC introduced its new two-year YTS in 1986. This was intended to be a quality scheme and a permanent and integral part of the system of training for young people. How the new scheme evolves in the future, particularly given demographic changes and a shortage of young workers in the 1990s, remains to be seen.

THE WORKSHOP

The particular YOP scheme I studied, which I will call Seafield, was a training workshop. The negative image of training workshops in general was somewhat mitigated in the case of Seafield which was a model scheme and something of an MSC showpiece, and at least in the initial stages of its existence it had the reputation of being able to place large numbers of its graduates in jobs, meaning it could attract 'quality' trainees. On balance, the workshop contained a fairly ordinary selection of working-class young Scots.

The workshop was actually three workshops, each in different parts of the building and with separate staff. 'Knitwear' was exclusively for girls, each trainee having access to her own knitting machine and trained to produce hats, scarves, jumpers and socks. Here there were three supervisors. Boys were apportioned either to the 'Paintshop' where they learned the basics of the decorating trade, or the 'Joinery shop'. Boys' workshops had two supervisors each.

On their first day at 'work' each trainee was given a written list of rules.

Hours   8.15–4.15 Monday to Friday.

Clock in   If you are over three minutes late (8.18), 15 minutes will
             be docked from your wages. If you are over 18 minutes
             late (8.33) 30 minutes and so on.

Lunch	30 minutes (a hooter sounds).
Teabreak	2 x 10 minutes (not allowed to leave the workshop).
Absence	Have to phone in first day off.
Sickness	Over the year, 3 separate days are allowed without a doctor's line.
Holidays	Over the year, 12 days' paid holiday; 5 days of which must be taken at Christmas and New Year plus 10 public holidays.
Discipline	Warning system. Oral then written warning. All start on one month's trial. Can be dismissed anytime.
Wages	£23.

Management were young and progressive and were already anticipating the shift from YOP to YTS and gearing themselves towards being a Mode B scheme. A 'trainee contract' was drawn up and provides some insight into the aims of the workshop and its general ethos. The following are extracts from it.

Seafield is set up to give trainees the best possible preparation for a working life.

It's a place to improve your chance of getting a good job by working hard and following the advice of your supervisor.

It provides:

training, help with problems, help in looking for jobs.

Seafield will help you develop the qualities employers seek – honesty, enthusiasm, effort, reliability, realism, acceptance of authority (accepting someone else will be giving the orders and understanding why you have to do what is asked).

Trainees have to:

attend interviews, attend college, attend outdoor trips (to develop extra confidence and skills), look at a newspaper every day, visit the job centre once a week (the day you forget to do this is the day someone else gets the job you could have had).

Personal presentation – you will be expected to look clean and smart. You will get a personal report every month. Your progress will be assessed and you will be told how you match up to the above.

There was a taken-for-granted assumption that Seafield worked and that the reason it worked was because of 'discipline'. It was a word you heard a lot at Seafield; I had heard that Seafield was 'strict' before I arrived. I had been there for less than a week when two people (separately) pulled me aside to justify it.

Cath (knitwear supervisor):
In this place, the skills they learn are more or less redundant – at least for the girls – all we can give them here is work discipline. If we can send them out of here with a reference saying they've been punctual and hardworking, then this is actually quite a lot. It does help them get jobs. Seafield kids do get jobs.

Joe: The best we can do for them is to be able to say 'he attended', 'he was punctual', 'he worked hard', and a reference that says that'll get them jobs. It's a lot.

SOME METHODOLOGICAL CONSIDERATIONS

Altogether I spent five months in the workshop, two-and-a-half months with boys and two-and-a-half months with girls. Although points of method are discussed throughout the book (I mention my acceptance into workshops in my discussion of each workshop), it will be useful to make a few remarks here.

Participant observation seemed to be the method best suited to understanding the culture of these young people. Roberts (1975) argues: 'The advantages of participant observation lie in the quality of knowledge about the field which it yields. The researcher gets to know both the intimate surface of his [/her] "field" and also how the real world runs under the surface. He [/she] picks up the "informal" as well as the formal culture' (Roberts 1975: 246, my brackets). For my purposes the advantages of using participant observation far outweighed the disadvantages. The disadvantages, however, should not be dismissed. The problematic issues are well known: the way in which the presence of the participant observer influences events; the problems of analysing data, and so on. The extent to which it is possible to know how far empathy with subjects clouds judgement, or the extent to which it is possible to know how much events are affected by the presence of the researcher are limited. I did take certain precautions while still in the situation (for example, continually assessing my impact on situations, watching young people's behaviour from afar, asking my closest friends towards the end of my research how they first saw me and reacted to me, how they thought others did and how much they thought I had changed the situation). What I have tried to do for the reader here is explicitly to write myself into the research to allow people a certain amount of insight into my role and character in the workshop, to create room for people to assess for themselves my involvement in the situation.

In the workshop itself, I decided not to use a tape recorder. In a situation where eating natural yogurt for lunch would have set you apart as an outsider, there would have been little hope of acceptance for someone trying to record conversations. In the event, I would also have felt extremely uncomfortable with a notebook and pencil. I used none of these props and relied heavily on memory. I wrote nothing in the workshop. I developed a technique whereby if something cropped up that I wanted to remember, I would distance myself from the group at a time when nothing much was happening and recall it in my head. I remembered key words. By the end of my time in the workshop, I could recall whole long conversations with ease. This was by far the most significant skill I developed in the workshop.

My 'data' took the form of a daily dairy in which I recorded daily events. I wrote 'key incidents' in a complete form, and constructed biographies of key characters. I participated in the workshop as someone slightly older and I made firm friends with several of the girls and felt close to them and their culture. Some of the main insights into their lives I learned outside the workshop, waiting for the gates to open, in the clocking-in room, walking home or walking to the shops at lunchtime. I spent a lot of time in the toilets smoking and passing round 'fly' cigarettes or standing on the balcony doing the same. I felt I knew a lot about how they lived outside the workshop.

I was close to a number of boys too but in a different way. I observed them in the way the teenage girls did. I knew very little about what they did outside the workshop or about their families and their relationships with them. My way of relating to them was in a bantering, jokey way and I never felt I got to the bottom of their culture in the same way that I did with girls. For example, I knew how it felt to have sexist comments directed at me as a woman and I knew and had insight into how girls really felt about boys. With boys, when they made sexist comments about girls, when they appeared to relate to them only as sex objects, I was never sure how deep this went – what they actually wanted from girls. It is information like this that boys do not give up easily and I suspect that in order to find out you have to be one, and I was not. It is certainly a limitation of my study.

In Seafield, girls and boys inhabited different worlds. They occupied different space, and did different jobs. The way they responded to what was offered differed as well. And to do justice to their separate worlds needed separate studies. I had not always intended that my study should take this form. At many stages, alternatives were more tempting, quicker, neater (theoretically and methodologically) and would have been personally less telling. Following other cultural studies, I could have concentrated only on the responses of youth in their daily struggle against 'authority'. One week into Seafield, however, had me thoroughly preoccupied by gender and concerned about the way teenage boys discussed and related to teenage girls. An understanding of gender seemed imperative.

A purely feminist study at the cultural level also seemed an attractive option. As mentioned, existing literature on youth culture is largely about boys. A piece focusing primarily on women and highlighting the sexism of schemes and outlining the separate fate teenage girls meet at the hands of both authority and boys, could have helped right this balance. Yet, however sexist teenage boys were, being around them continually for months made it very difficult for me to downplay or ignore the enterprising nature of their behaviour at Seafield. Ultimately, the decision to study the workshop in its entirety seemed an obvious one.

I tried to look behind the easy-going happy facade that this particular group of young people presented to the world and tried to uncover deeper aspects of their lives, the parts of their lives which tend to slip through the net of traditional social science methodology, which do not filter up and become part of taken-for-granted social knowledge until much later. And this was partly possible for me for a whole series of unexpected (and not so unexpected) reasons.

Who I was in the world in general structured and eased my acceptance in Seafield. Yet who I was (to working-class teenagers) was, at first, unknown to me (and a major source of initial anxiety). My acceptance happened on the basis of assumptions made about me which I did not understand until much later. My role was fixed by things I was not immediately aware were important. In my first weeks there I was asked a few key questions. On the basis of my answers my image was built. It stuck for all of the time I was at Seafield.

The first and most important question was whether or not I had a boyfriend (they assumed I was childless and unmarried). That I did not was probably the biggest single factor which put me on the same footing as themselves. I was no threat. Had I had a boyfriend (or been married) my research would have taken a different form. Next, they asked how much money I got to attend Seafield. My grant, I told them, was slightly higher than their wage. This was disagreeable but not much of a threat. They asked what my father did. He was a bricklayer and this did nothing to set me apart. They placed my accent after a week.

'Yer no' fae Edinburgh ur ye?'

'Bit, yer no' fae Glasga' either. Yer fae wan o' tha' places in between. Bet yer fae Whitburn.'

Whitburn is two miles away from where I was born. They placed me more efficiently than any sociologist could have done. I was assumed to be young. I didn't wear make up and was not so familiar with their culture as I had once been. They thought me simple and naïve. But my naïveté was more than made up for by my kindness. (Participant observers do anything to keep in with people!) And I was generally liked. I became integrated (more or less) as one of them. Their behaviour was not modified for me more than it would have been for any other.

Yet, despite being accepted and in many ways familiar with their culture, I was constantly aware of the enormous problems of knowing. I touched (and could only touch) one tiny part of their lives. I could easily have spent five months in Seafield knowing them in a completely different way and on a completely different level. What I ultimately came to think of as the important things about their culture could have remained hidden.

Indeed, for the first few weeks, until I had made friends of my own, like most newcomers (I found out later), I lived in isolation. I had little idea of what their lives were really like and what was really happening. I barely remember the content of early conversations. They were utterly different from the ones which filled my days later. What I do remember are general impressions. Trainees seemed confident, happy and easy-going. This image of them did not last. By the end of my time there, these impressions had been completely transformed. Each and every one of them seemed to carry around a burden of misery. Indeed, a lot of my time in the workshop was spent unpicking the painful and difficult conditions of their lives.

IMPLICATIONS OF GENDER

The lack of literature and detailed study of this group is testimony enough that their culture is little known about. As McRobbie and Garber say (1975: 222): '... girl culture, from our preliminary investigations, is so well insulated as to operate to effectively exclude not only other "undesirable" girls – but also buys, adults, teachers and researchers.' This group have simply never had a voice. For working-class boys there have always been traditional (albeit limited) ways out. There are tried and tested escape routes to the middle class and to situations which provide opportunities for becoming articulate. There are outlets for sharing experiences which then become better known about and more widely appreciated. The culture of working-class girls, by contrast, is deeply hidden. The socialisation process is one from which few escape. The number who escape to new situations of independence and confidence and to positions which do afford them time, space, money and the skills required to reflect on and to want to share an analysis of their own culture, are minute. It is this culture that I have tried to unravel here.

NOTES

1   See in particular *Resistance Through Rituals* (Hall and Jefferson (eds.): 1975).
2   See in particular *Working Class Youth Cultures* (Mungham and Pearson: 1976).
3   The piece of empirical work that I know of that best attempts this is *Brothers* (1983) by Cynthia Cockburn. Again, it is worth noting the sympathetic insight into the worlds of her male respondents that Cockburn, a female researcher, was able to achieve.
4   See Markall (1982) for discussion of the Job Creation Scheme.
5   See Goldstein (1984).

1

GIRLS AMONG BOYS

In the previous chapter I talked briefly about how I conducted my research. Here I want to discuss in more detail how I came to be accepted in the paintshop. This section says as much about how girls fare in male workplaces as it does about anything else.

NO PLACE FOR GIRLS

> *Me:* Do girls do painting and joinery too?
>
> *Jan* (training officer):
> Not really. Well actually, we do have a girl starting. It's our first and none of us is very keen. To tell you the truth, I'm always suspicious of girls who claim they want to paint. They usually only want to do it for really flightly reasons. Anyway, there are so many boys desperate for apprenticeships and experience that that has to be my priority. We just don't have places for girls. But this girl was so determined to paint that we decided to let her.

My first few days in Seafield were anxious. I spent them observing trainees from the safe distance of the office. I watched people come and go, tried to discover how the place worked and to imagine a role for myself. Hopes of studying boys and girls together vanished in the realisation of how complete sex segregation was in the workshop. Girls and boys occupied different parts of the building, the division of labour was by gender (boys painted, girls knitted), lunch times and breaks were staggered in time and the sexes never (officially) met. The experience of being a girl was utterly different from that of being a boy. Boys' workshops were cold, male and uncomfortable. Upstairs, girls knitted in warmth and feminine comfort. Working with girls seemed like a possibility. My first real contact with boys reinforced a growing feeling that studying them was going to be impossible.

It was my third day in the office. I tentatively approached Tam (the supervisor in the paintshop) to ask if he would show me around. I reminded him I was being careful not to be seen as a member of staff or as an official of any kind.

Tam: Right you lot. Ah want ye's tae meet somebody. This is a Miss Anne Stafford. She's the new assistant here, an' she's here tae keep an eye oan you lot. An' ye's better treat her wi' the same respect as ye's treat me. Dae ye's hear, or ye's 'll huv me tae answer tae.

Next day I made one last ditch attempt to find a way to study boys.

Me: Tam, dae ye' think it would be possible for me tae spend some time in your workshop. Dae ye' think ye' could find something for me to do?

Tam: Ah dunno'. See, these are boys' workshops. There's no' an awffy lot fur a lassie tae dae here. It wid be handy if ye' could type or something'. It'd be handy tae get somebody tae type ma estimates, but a' the rest is boys' work.

The paintshop had been set up as a place for boys. It was not a place for girls. Tam could almost conceive of my presence there as an office worker, but as a painter, with status equal to that of the boys, it was unthinkable.

The structure of the workshop, its general ethos, was set up as near as possible to resemble a real workplace. Nowhere was this ideal more rigorously pursued than in the paintshop. In real decorating firms (limited by constraints of the market) there is little time for niceties such as training girls. And it did not happen here. The aim in the workshop was to reproduce workplace conditions and to turn out trainees fit for the world of work. It meant that the paintshop was as off-putting to girls as a male workplace would have been.

TRISH AND ME: A FROSTY RECEPTION

Traditionally, participant observers succeed when they have something to offer and my fortunes changed when this became possible for me. My access to the paintshop was blocked because I was a girl. Trish (mentioned at the beginning of this chapter) negotiated her own access. It was eventually and reluctantly given. No-one wanted her there and certainly no-one wanted her there alone. I leapt at the opportunity of being the second girl in the paintshop.

We met for the first time outside the paintshop at eight fifteen one Monday morning, too terrified to go in. It was an unlikely alliance. Yet throughout the two-and-a-half months I spent in the paintshop we were inseparable. For either of us alone, the situation would have been unbearable.

My experience of the paintshop was structured through Trish, her experience was linked to mine. Interpretations of what was happening we worked out together. Analysing boys' relations with each other and with us was our full-time occupation. My age and (slightly) more confident air were important in coping with initial hostility. And without her I would never have come to such a close understanding of the culture of boys. Trish fed me cues and brought me faster to acceptable behaviour. She gave me legitimation in the eyes of boys that I would have found difficult to obtain for myself. And what was an alliance based on need and dependency

ended in friendship based on respect for our two very different ways of life
– a friendship which unfortunately lasted only as long as our time together
in the workshop, before our different lifestyles took us along very different
paths.

We moved inside the paintshop when the hooter went. We met a solid
block of silence and hostility. It took a long time to unravel and understand
the forces which created this atmosphere and which indicated the extent of
the threat that we posed to boys by our presence. Supervisors and boys
alike seemed unable to relate to girls in this setting. For my part, I wanted
nothing more than to walk out of the workshop and never come back. Our
first days were a nightmare. We were tested, tried and challenged from the
beginning. Our first obstacle was Tam. Persuading him to allow us to stay
seemed like an impossible task.

Tam: Right you lassies, fur the first few weeks ye'll no' get near a
paintbrush. Ye'll be cleanin' up. Then we'll see how ye' shape up.
Ah'm pitten' ye's oan cleanin' door handles. A few days oan that an'
ah'll bet ye' never get paint oan a door handle again.

For the first few days we did not see a paintbrush. We hardly saw a boy!
Tam's initial tactic for dealing with our presence was to keep us apart from
boys and pretend that we did not exist. We spent these days with steel wool
and scrapers, removing paint from every door handle in the building. This
was interspersed with breaks in the canteen where we were met by a wall
of boys; stony, silent, hostility. No-one spoke a word. We very obviously
disrupted all of their usual daily interaction. Boys were embarrassed and
unable to say anything or to carry on as normal. I found the situation
unbearable. Trish, though, was more relaxed about it than I was.

Trish: Oct, they'll get used tae us.

To me there seemed no way boys could or would want to relate to us. Tam
escalated rather than minimised what was happening. Our first few days
were confusing and embarrassing. It took a long time to understand the
deep-rooted reasons for their single-minded determination to keep us out.
And it was Trish who first (intuitively) grasped the situation and who first
took steps to counteract it. What was obvious from the beginning was that
so much of the hostility towards us was expressed in terms of our
(threatening) sexuality.

For example, on our very first morning, as we entered the workshop we
were immediately given new overalls. For boys, putting on overalls was
neutral. For us, in front of a sea of staring boys, it felt sexual, embarrassing
and degrading. And from then on, not for one moment were we allowed
to forget that we were girls, that we were sex objects and that we were out
of place.

Tam: Right you lassies, when ye's come intae this wee back room, ah
want ye's in here two at a time. Dae ye's understand. Ah dinnae want
ye's in here yersel's.

Trish and I were both angry at this remark.

Trish: Diz he think we're gaunnae rape him or some'at?

Tam's nervousness about us was a concern about boys and reflected generally-held ideas about them and their unformed and as yet uncontrollable sexuality. Stereotypical ideas about sexuality also extended to include Tam himself. Embarrassed about the above remark, he tried to justify it to me later.

Tam: Ah dunno' whit ye' made o'that remark ah made earlier. But, call me auld fashioned if ye' like – but ye's cannae deny it – ye's ur'attractive wee lassies. Dae ye's ken whit ah mean?

At the beginning of our second week, Tam took us out on our first job. It was something of a breakthrough and our first taste of 'real' work. Of course the breakthrough came with a sting in the tail. It did little to make me feel more optimistic about our situation.

Tam: Right, Elvis, Pete, Punk Pete, Mo, in the van, we're gaun't oot tae a job in L.... Anne an' the wee lassie tae. Take yer' stuff wi' ye', ye'll no' be back – handbags tae, fur those o' ye' that hae them.

Out on the job, Trish and I felt so uncomfortable that we spent our first few lunches wandering the streets. The laughter and easy banter we heard from the end of the hall on our return stopped abruptly as we appeared in the doorway. Their 'normal' way of relating (it seemed) could not take place in front of girls.

Ideas generally held in society, ideas about women, men and sexuality, structure the exclusion of women from male workplaces generally. And because the workshop emulated rather than challenged what happened in real workplaces, these ideas also organised the way Seafield operated. Schemes like these took on employers' definitions of the problem and worked towards fitting young people for the world of work. Trainees themselves were seen to be the problem and this concerned their morality and sexuality too. Indeed, the problem of containing and controlling them came to be about controlling and containing their forming and problematic sexuality. A vital factor built into the disciplinary structure of Seafield had to do with and was built around generally-held ideas about teenage sexuality and how to contain it.

In Seafield the sexes were kept apart, which had many implications. Keeping boys and girls apart created the kind of workplace environment around which could be built a boys' culture that was exclusive of girls. Boys were brought to feel that they were doing work that was male – work that girls could not do. They could feel positive about themselves in relation to and at the expense of girls. Sex segregation was the basis upon which was built the superiority of boys and the subordination of girls. It created the basis upon which an atmosphere could be generated where daily interaction was exclusive of girls, indeed, was inappropriate when girls were around. Our presence challenged a very basic tenet upon which the acceptance of Seafield by boys was based. Our acceptance meant, on the one hand, convincing Tam that our sex and morality were not a problem, and on the other being able to work there without undermining the notion that work in the workshop was too difficult for girls. To me it seemed like an impossible task. I had reckoned without the determination of Trish.

TAM'S LASSIES

I felt increasing pessimism. If the situation continued, our days in the workshop seemed numbered. My despair at the situation sprung from my own ideals, for acceptance, for me, implied acceptance as equals. Trish, much less pessimistic, had other ideas, and her strategy was effective (though not one I would have used myself). She determinedly set about creating a role for herself that was not on the same basis as boys but rather one which meant behaving in ways that were feminine. Her aim was to fit in as a girl, and she used feminine ways of turning sexism to her (short-term) advantage. For example, Tam turned up at breaktime. There was no spare cup for him.

Trish: Ah'll jist finish ma tea Tam then ah'll make you wan.

Trish's first aim was to win round Tam and she set about it by trying to make herself as pleasant and as helpful as possible. She was pleased to be allowed to do the smallest and most menial of tasks, tasks that boys would never have done. She made paste for the wallpaperers, just as they needed it and without being asked. She continually swept shavings, wiped up, passed scrapers. I busied myself in much the same way but less avidly. Trish tried to make herself acceptable and indispensable as a woman. She softened the harsher aspects of men-only workplaces and in an astoundingly short space of time she was indispensable and her presence (and mine) taken for granted. Suddenly, and for reasons about which I felt dubious, staying seemed all too possible.

Trish had become Tam's assistant. In womanly ways she made his life in the workshop more comfortable, making tea for him and keeping the place tidy. He fell into entrusting her with tasks he would not have entrusted to the boys.

Tam: Trish, you see tae the keys. Lock up and make sure sure everything is pit away.

Tam: Trish, make sure tha' laddies dinnae make a hash o' things in there.

Tam: Make us a cup o' tea, eh Trish?

Trish's tactics had paid off. And she had been successful in another way as well. Trish became widely respected as a 'good girl'. She was aloof from boys and indeed ignored their presence. In doing this she quickly alleviated Tam's worst fears while at the same time dissociated herself from the reputation of girls in knitwear who were generally held to be 'wild'. Trish and I became known as 'Tam's lassies'.

Tam (to me in confidence): She'll be a' right eh, the wee lassie? She's quiet, thank God. God knows whit ah wid huv done wi' a wild yin.

Any amount o' wild laddies ah kin handle, ah could knock ony laddie intae shape, bit ah widnae know whit tae dae wi' a wild lassie. We now had a basis for staying and were beginning to feel like we belonged. My heart positively soared at this conversation.

I asked Tam about the up-and-coming workshop football match. Naïvely I asked if girls went as well.

Joe (supervisor in joinery):

Naw, we've decided no' tae let them go. They got goin' the last time an' ah'm tellin' ye' they were wild. They're jist no' interested in fitba' tha' lassies. The last time they didnae even watch the match. They spent the whole time wrestlin' wi' each other oan the grass. They really waste it fur themselves tha' lassies. So they're no' gettin' goin' this time.

Tam: Aye, bit ma lassies are goin' Joe, ah'll make sure o' that.

Trish had done well. In my own way so had I.

Tam (in confidence):

Ye've done well. Done me a favour actually – oan the wee lassie. Ah'll tell ye' the truth, ah didnae want her. If she'd come hersel' ah couldnae huv' coped. Ah wiz gaunnae gie her a month's trial, then she wiz oot. Noo she'll fit in, she'll dae her year noo.

TRISH THE PAINTER

I was relieved to be able to stay, even on this basis. But in accepting this I had in fact badly underestimated Trish. She had more ambitious plans for herself than merely being Tam's domestic. Her tactics were more sophisticated than I had originally given her credit for. The disquiet I felt about her initial role was dispelled in the realisation that hers was an ongoing struggle, part of a continual effort on her part to better her position in the workshop. Trish knew what she wanted. She wanted to be a painter and she intuitively knew the obstacles to be crossed, the painstaking work that had to be done to get there. When she was established at one stage, she pushed further.

When Tam did eventually allow Trish to paint, she proved competent with a paintbrush and as quick to learn as any boy. Her jobs were always well done and meticulous. She never left a gloss brush in water or failed to clean an emulsion brush. She always used the appropriate brush. Her jobs were well prepared, sanded, all the holes filled. She slowly gained the reputation of being a good painter. We progressed to 'real' jobs alongside boys and Tam began to imagine a new role for Trish.

Tam: The wee lassie's gaunnae make it. She's gaunnae be wan o' them. An' ah'll make her a damned good painter. There's nae other scheme aboot here wid take oan a lassie. Ah huv'. She'll no' get a joab, bit wan day, when she's got a hoose o' her ain, by god, she'll kin dae it up, fae top tae bottom. An' if she's goat tradesmen in, by Christ, she'll know whit's gaun' oan.

When the boys too started to relax around us, we felt we had really arrived. Because Trish had initially been 'cool' around them, and related to them in their own terms, they slowly began to accept her as someone who was sexually neutral, a sister and a tomboy. The role suited me too.

Our biggest breakthrough, though, happened when two new boys started and Trish and I were no longer the newest trainees. They started into a situation where girls were painters. Indeed, it was Trish and I who were initially responsible for their initiation. They looked to us as sources of information and looked to us for tips.

> *Tam:* You new laddies, go wi' the lassies. They'll show ye's whit tae dae.

We spent the first day with them chatting, at the same time doing heavy manual jobs. We confidently carried benches down from the canteen, sanded them down and varnished them. That *we* were experienced *they* took for granted. They questioned us about the workshop, chatted about their lives, about music, about clothes. *Our* long struggle to be allowed to do this they knew nothing about. And at this stage Tam's ideas for Trish progressed another stage.

> *Tam* (casually to Trish):
> There's a job gaun' as a sales assistant in the M... paint shop. Ur' ye' wantin' tae go in fur it?
> *Trish* (emphatically):
> Nut!
> *Tam:* Aye, that's whit ah thought. Ah jist thought ah'd ask ye'.

Next day.

> *Mo* (to Trish):
> Did ye' no' want that job?
> *Trish:* Naw!
> *Mo:* Aye, that's whit Tam said. He says ye've goat yer heart set oan bein' a painter.
> *Trish:* If ah'd wanted a joab in a shop, ah widnae huv' come here.

Tam now had aspirations for Trish as an apprentice. His thoughts were on the publicity for Seafield and the status of having been responsible for turning out one of the first girl apprentices in the decorating trade locally.

TRISH BLOWS IT: A QUESTION OF MORALITY

To fit into the workshop, Trish had to participate in the daily culture of the paintshop in a way that was sexually neutral. She created a role for herself that was daughter to Tam, sister to the boys and as a girl set apart from and better than girls in knitwear. Keeping everyone happy was a balancing act which became more difficult to manage as time in the workshop went on.

Tam liked Trish best when she was new, awkward and unconfident, when she was ignoring boys and servicing him. In the long term this was untenable. As we became more established and more confident about being allowed to stay, and as we increased the amount of contact we had with boys, our relationship with them changed. We inhibited boys less and less. And after a time, their daily interaction seemed barely affected by us. Soon, boys were swearing, fighting, sloshing each other with paintbrushes and discussing girls, whether we were there or not. Gradually, we were sucked more and more into their culture and we began to participate in the general carry-on, discussing everything from politics to nights out.

But our new-found confidence with boys brought its own costs. The double standard once more raised its ugly head. What was acceptable behaviour for boys was not acceptable for Trish, and the difference was to do with morality. Disruptive behaviour from boys was seldom connected to questions about their sexual identity (if it was, it enhanced it). For Trish, her behaviour was always closely tied to questions about her morality. For example, when Pete chased Mo with a paintbrush, this was sexually neutral, the implications of being caught relatively minor. When Trish chased Peter, a sexual motive was assumed. She appeared 'cheap', immoral and consequences of *her* being caught would have been severe.

Trish learned fast when it came to grasping what was and what was not acceptable behaviour. Some lessons, though, she had to learn the hard way. To be allowed to stay, she had to be seen to be sexually neutral. The importance of this lesson she did not learn fast enough and the learning of it almost had disastrous consequences. Tam picked up her increasing ease with boys faster than she learned the importance of hiding it. Inevitably perhaps, as Trish's confidence grew, as her relationships with boys eased, she lost sight of her earlier caution. She began to see them as potential boyfriends. She settled on Elvis and set about letting him know she was interested. Her initial role of being cool and disinterested was replaced by a new one. Trish became giggly, coy and embarrassed when Elvis was around and more and more preoccupied by him. This change in her behaviour had widespread implications. For it was not only Elvis, but all of the boys, who treated her differently. Trish ceased to be a sister to them. She became a sex object and available. The workshop buzzed with interest. If Elvis did not succeed, it was obvious that more boys were waiting in the wings to take his place. Sexual feelings were around and Tam picked up on it fast. His worst fears were beginning to be realised.

I stayed off work one day. When I came back Trish was subdued and sulky.

    Me: Whit's up wi' ye'?

    Trish: Nuthin'.

Eventually she told me what had happened.

    Trish: Tam took me off workin' wi' the laddies yesterday. Ah spent the whole day workin' by masel'. It wiz horrible.

Trish felt punished. She knew Tam was aware of her increasing interest in boys. The situation worsened as the afternoon progressed. Later that day, seeing Trish working by herself, Frankie (in a genuinely friendly way) had gone over to the window where Trish was working to have a chat. Tam had walked in at that moment, rushed over to Frankie and pushed him roughly away.

Trish: Tam says ah wiz tae leave the laddies alane. He says ah distract them. He says he wisnae accusin' me o' anythin' an' that if anythin' did happen it wid likely be their fault, but he telt me ah wisnae tae flirt wi' them or ah wid lose ma job.

Ah telt him it wisnae fair, ah hudnae done onythin', it wiz them. He says he ken't that, but ah wisnae tae encourage them.

She said to me later, with great bitterness:

Trish: It's no' fair. Ah git the row fur whit they dae. They kin sleep wi' a thousand burds an' it's OK. You jist need tae look at wan o' them an' yer a slag.

Trish did flirt, but boys' behaviour in relation to her was no better. Yet when things did get out of hand (in Tam's terms), boys' behaviour went unsanctioned. Her behaviour was judged on a different standard, her morality was questioned and her reputation was badly affected.

After a long build-up (the details of which are the substance of another chapter) and during which excitement mounted, Trish did eventually go out with Elvis. It happened only once. It only took once for Trish to realise how vital it was to be seen in the workshop as someone who was sexually neutral. The advantage of this were sharply brought home to Trish on her first date.

Trish: If ah go oot wi' a guy fae here, the rest'll a' ken aboot me. Elvis'll talk, ah ken he will. An' ah'll no' know whit tae dae. Things wid be awffy different at work, he'd be watchin' me a' the time when ah'd be jist talkin' tae the other laddies. Elvis is a barry guy an' that, an' we'd a barry time, bit, ah dunno' whit's wrong wi' me, ah jist dinnae want tae go oot wi' him noo.

To be taken seriously as a worker meant that Trish could not have a boyfriend in the workshop; more than this, it meant not showing interest in boys as boyfriends at all. Trish learned this lesson the hard way. The learning of it came almost too late.

Next morning, Trish was called into Jan's office and reprimanded.

Tam: Look hen, ah dinnae care whit ye' dae ootside, ye' kin go oot wi' whoever ye' like, bit jist keep it oot o' the workshop, an' dinnae let it affect yer work.

Had she continued going around with Elvis, her stay in the workshop would have been short. She stopped in the nick of time and Tam and Trish settled into some kind of uneasy compromise. In Tam's eyes, Trish had blown it, she'd let him down badly. She was no longer 'Tam's lassie', special and set aside from girls in knitwear. She had, however, established herself enough as a painter to be allowed to stay. She worked alongside boys, participating in their daily banter and conversation. Tam had lost his high expectations of her as a model trainee, but by this time she was established and taken for granted nonetheless. Her new position in the workshop I think she preferred, and I certainly felt easier about it.

Changes between Trish and myself were affected by and also reflected changes in the process of our acceptance into the workshop generally. It was, as I have already said, an unlikely relationship. Born out of need, it ended in respect and friendship and it developed through many inter-mediate stages. Initially we were both nervous and at sea. In terms of confidence, at that stage, I had the edge on Trish. Faced with blanket hostility, my age and experience in the world (in some things), and because I carried with me a positive image of myself from friends, all meant that I was slightly better equipped to meet a vanload of hostile boys or a room full of silent ones. Without a doubt, at a time when Trish was nervous and unsure of herself, my presence helped her through a situation she might otherwise have been unable to cope with.

Trish: That's the thing that amazes me aboot you Anne. Ye' dinnae get bothered by nuthin'. Ye' kin dae anythin' wi'oot gettin' embar-rassed. Ye're dead confident. Ah get embarrassed at the least wee thing. Ah'd huv' run right hame the first day if ye'd no' been there.

On another occasion.

Me: Trish, ah'll no' be in the morra'. Ah huv' tae go tae the university.

I wanted to attend a local conference on the state.

Trish: God ye're jokin', ye' cannae leave me masel' wi' the laddies.

Trish: Mind an' be here at ten past eight. Ah'll wait oan ye' ootside the gate.

Trish: Ah've tae go up fur paint, gaunnae chum me?

Trish: Ah'm gaunnae meet ma ma at break tae gie her ma pay, ye' gaunnae chum me?

This pattern changed and it changed because of the way we ultimately came to be seen by the boys. The description of this provides, I think, a good illustration of how women's identities and images of themselves are formed in relation to and through men.

It became obvious from early on that boys were interested (sexually) in Trish and not in me. She was seen to be good-looking, 'cool', 'hard to get'. Having me as a girlfriend would have impressed no-one. I was not held to be attractive. Rather, boys thought I was a bit slow and naïve. I was always Trish's nice but unattractive pal. As the boys came to define her as popular, her confidence in relation to me increased. My standing fell, and the more sought-after she became, the more she became independent from me and the more she came to define what happened between us. Trish took on board definitions of herself from boys and related to me accordingly.

Trish: See you Anne, ye'r that naïve.

Trish: God Anne, ye'r slow oan the uptake.

From the situation of her being dependent on me in order to function in the workshop at all, as our friendship developed in relation to boys I was the one that came to be treated (and felt myself to be) young, naïve and uninteresting.

Trish: 'Ur you eighteen yet?

Me: Ah'm twenty-four.

Trish: Ye're nut, ye're a fuckin' liar.

Me: Ah'm no'. Ah'm twenty-four, honest.

Trish: God, ah cannae believe it, ye' dinnae look it. Nae offence but, it must be 'cause ye're sae wee, an' 'cause ye' dinnae wear any make-up.

At the time, I was actually even older.

Trish: Hoi, guess whit age she is?

Kenny: Sixteen.

Mo: Seventeen.

Craigie: Eighteen.

Trish: Tell them.

Me: Ah'm twenty-four.

Kenny: Aye, ye'r arse, don' gies it!

On another occasion, before Trish did know my age.

Trish: Dae ye' ever go tae the dancin'?

Me: Aye, sometimes.

Trish: Dae ye'? Dae ye' no' hae trouble gettin' in, 'cause ye'r sae wee?

Me: (adamantly):

Nut!

I had been effectively pushed into a subordinate role in relation to Trish and it was now she who offered advice and was protective.

Trish: Huv; ye' goat a boyfriend?

Me: Nut!

Trish: Ah ken't ye' widnae. Bet ye're the type that never bothers wi' boys.

Me: Naw no' really.

Trish (sympathetically):

S'funny, some lassies ur' jist like that. Ah quite like laddies masel'.

Had I started in the boys' workshop without Trish it is impossible to know what my role would have been. What I do know is that being seen to be Trish's pal gave me access, legitimation and closeness to boys' culture. Trish initiated me, protected me, pointed out aspects of teenage culture that were new and reminded me of aspects that I had forgotten. These were the benefits of my friendship with Trish and the role I had in the workshop. On the other side, the costs were high. To take on this role meant putting myself into the most personally undermining situation I had been in for ten years. And as I became more integrated, it became harder.

Mo: Stafford's goat oan that gobbin' jersey again.

Pete: You eatin' again Stafford? Dae ye' never gie ye'r stomach a rest?

Along with the sheer hard work and the early start each morning, the daily writing up of notes meant that by the end of my time there I felt flattened. The workshop has really gotten to me. The cumulative effect of hard work, authoritarian structures, sexism, boredom and the relentless task of writing up notes, because I'm too exhausted to go out at night means that I feel at the very limits of my endurance. I feel as if I've suffered a massive crash of confidence, about class, about gender, about my appearance and my friendships. I've been out of the workshop for a week now and I'm only beginning to feel human again.

I left the paintshop feeling exhausted and depressed. Trish, on the other hand, through her popularity with boys, increased her status, independence and confidence particularly in relation to me. The benefits to her, though, were temporary and fragile and were bought at the high cost of being ultimately undermined in the relationships she did have with boys. I shall discuss this fully in the section on sexuality.

2

THE POLITICS OF THE PAINTSHOP

The paintshop housed fifteen boys and two supervisors (Tam and Robbie). It was a huge room, every inch a male workplace and more of a stockroom than a place to work. It stored scaffolding, tins of paint, ladders, paint-brushes, dust-sheets and tools. It was cold and bare, the walls were covered with graffiti. People reported here in the morning to leave coats and possessions and to put on overalls. It was here that the tasks of the day were given out.

I have already discussed Seafield as a model scheme, and it was in the paintshop that this reputation was formed. Painters had the image of being well-behaved and hard working. In the workshop in general, painters had a high profile. Boys in white overalls were everywhere, busily transporting ladders and scaffolding, rushing up and down stairs, transporting tin after tin of paint, loading and unloading the van. Groups of boys would descend on one room after another and transform it with earnest determination. They seemed competent and mature.

Part of the reputation of the workshop was based on its very real (at the time) ability to place boys in jobs and apprenticeships with local firms. This was widely attributed to providing boys with 'a bloody good training'. Superficially this seemed true. Reality was more complicated.

TAM'S PERSONAL ASPIRATIONS

For anyone spending time in the paintshop, it was tempting to attribute the hard-working, well-disciplined atmosphere to the force of Tam's person-ality. Tam took the job of disciplining trainees more seriously than any other supervisor and the paintshop had a regime which was positively authoritarian. To understand 'Tam's rule' you need to know a little about his personal background.

Tam was working-class, a tradesman and nearing retirement. Most of his working life had been spent in the decorating trade. The job at Seafield must have come as something of a relief. He wholeheartedly embraced the aims and ideals of the workshop and the seriousness of his commitment was impressive. For example, some of the boys, Trish and myself had been painting a long corridor in a nearby church. We were there because a previous generation of YOPs from the workshop had already completed a piece of work there. Tam pulled me aside and beckoned me to follow him. He took me into the church proper and showed me the previous job. It was difficult to believe that it could have been done by a group of sixteen-year-olds. Long bannisters had been varnished, scaffolding had been raised, high ceilings painted, cornices were gold and perfectly painted. In the quiet of the church, Tam turned to me and said with real emotion: 'An' Ah did that wi' a bunch o' laddies.'

Tam had worked all his life as a manual worker, training apprentices to the highest standards. The 'lighter' job could have left him feeling demoralised, in that it represented a step down. Instead, Tam managed to make and to keep this job challenging and male. And for him, self-respect came from transforming and moulding a 'bunch o' laddies', unable even to find jobs, into a group of exceptional workers. For his own pride, he took his job and Seafield seriously.

> *Tam:* These laddies ah turn oot, if they'd beards and moustaches, if they looked a wee bit aulder, a' could pass them off as tradesmen, never mind bloody apprentices.

In the paintshop, then, supervisors were male and working-class, used to dealing with apprentices. Their own identities as men were tied up with manual work. Making the job culturally relevant for themselves meant recreating manual work conditions here. However, if the attempt in this particular workshop was to transmit practical skills in a similar way to the old apprenticeship system, this time it was mediated through YOP and there were important differences.

Tam saw his job both as passing on relevant practical skills and also as helping young people who were deprived. These ideological arrangements provided space and justification for a regime which, though understandable in terms of YOP ideology, was harsher even than the old apprenticeship system. At times it felt positively punitive.

TAM'S DISCIPLINE

In the paintshop, the limits of acceptable behaviour were narrowly defined and rigidly set. Order was kept in a regime partly based on fear. Tam going 'raj' was an unpleasant experience for even the toughest of boys. I would give a verbatim account of this but unfortunately (or fortunately, I am not sure which), as 'girls' Trish and I were excluded. We were always sent out of a room where Tam was about to loose his anger on boys. My accounts are second-hand.

> *Frankie:* See Fergy, he wiz six feet six, the toughest guy that's ever been here. See Tam, even had him greetin'. Tam could get anybody greetin'.

> *Mo:* Ye' want tae huv' seen Tam this mornin'. We were a' skivin' an'

in he walks an' catches us. Must huv' jist had a row wi' the missus or some'at 'cause he went completely berserk, fuckin' an' blindin' a' owr the place. Ah thought he wiz gaunni burst, an' his false eye jump oot. We were shitin' it.

Part of the effectiveness of Tam losing his temper stemmed from the fact that his outbursts were neither consistent nor predictable. Onslaughts directed at a whole group one day were directed at a single culprit the next. Behaviour which provoked a violent reaction one day would be ignored and passed over without comment the next. His behaviour was unpredictable. Boys had to be continually on their toes.

Tam was everyone's guardian angel, the watcher at everyone's back. When he left a room he never said when he would be back. His arrival was never announced; instead, he would creep up to a room and suddenly, he would be there. He turned up in the oddest of places at the oddest of times. Boys, for their part, took all the precautions they could, posting lookouts, misbehaving in ways which could be stopped at a moment's notice.

Tam knew boys skived. This was acceptable. Men in workplaces did this all the time. It was a game. It was, though, a game with limits. Sometimes Tam won by catching them and the repercussions were fairly minor; sometimes boys won by being clever enough to cover up and be caught at nothing. And sometimes the game got out of hand, transgressed the limits and repercussions were severe.

Tam had silently crept up to the paintshop door and caught Punk Pete 'keepin' shotty'. He prevented him warning the others. Tam was almost gleeful when he strolled into the workshop and caught all the boys on the hop, scurrying about picking up work just a few seconds too late.

Tam: Whit's gaun' oan in here?

The collective response was one of dumb silence. Tam went around everyone individually asking them to account for what they had been doing. Each stumbled to some kind of answer.

Tam: Whit've you been daein'?

Cogs: Cleanin' up.

Pete: Lookin' fur gloss.

Craigie: Cleanin' brushes.

Trish: Gettin' mair putty.

At this point, Tam's wrath was contained, his anger more ritual than real. At this stage he was merely pleased to have caught their lookout napping. Events took a more serious turn when, mid-sentence, he realised that one of the boys was missing.

Tam: Where's Wee Rab?

No reply. Tam's anger rapidly increased to danger point.

Tam (roaring at the top of his voice):
Where's Wee Rab?

Still no reply. Tam stormed out of the room and rushed upstairs to check if he was there. No sign. Tam returned in a rage. Wee Rab by now was standing in the paintshop. The atmosphere was heavy and tense. Tam's temper had reached danger level.

Tam: (roaring): Where have you been?

Wee Rab: Through the back, gettin' a drink o' water.

Tam knew and accepted that boys skived. So long as boys stopped as soon as Tam appeared he was satisfied. Deliberately to remain hidden while Tam charged around the workshop trying to find you was a gross violation of Tam's limits. It made Tam feel like a fool, that boys had massively undermined his authority. The incident with Wee Rab set him off on a rage which lasted for days and terrified all the boys. He shouted on and on at Wee Rab, on and on at all the boys. He wound himself up into a fervour. He accused them of being lazy, worthless, untrustworthy, thick and stupid, claiming they would never get jobs. And he rounded off the performance by suspending everyone. His parting shot was to me.

Tam: An' pit that in yer memoirs!

His anger spilled over into the next day. He suspended Punk Pete and Wee Rab again for some minor infringement. In all, Punk Pete was suspended four times that week, leaving him with a take-home pay of £9. Financially it had not been worth his while being in the workshop.

Apart from the atmosphere of outright fear which Tam so easily could create, there were other tactics he used to discipline boys. Sarcasm was one.

Tam: (gently): C'mere sonny, where's yer scraper?

Davy: Left it at hame.

Tam: (gently, with sarcasm): Ye've left it at hame? Well never mind, ye' kin jist supervise this job instead. You jist be in charge o' this job, eh?

Tam:(now roaring): Ye've left yer' scraper at hame. We'll ah've ah good fuckin' mind tae make ye' clock back oot an' get the fuckin' thing.

Tam's sense of humour was essentially linked to undermining boys and, for that matter, Trish and myself. For example, Trish and I had been standing on window ledges undercoating windows for the best part of two days. We were bored. Late on Friday afternoon, Tam paid us a surprise visit.

Tam: How are ye's gettin' oan? It's a real shame ye've been daein' this fur sae long. Ye's must be sick tae death o' this. Ye's look, like ye's need a change. Tell ye's what, ah'll gie ye's a wee change oan Monday. Ye's can gloss them a'!

On another occasion, Tam came in to find that someone had ruined the chamois cloth. They had left it soaking all night in water or in turps.

Tam: Right you lot. Who the fuck did this tae the cloth? Who did it? Cogs, whit dae ye' call this?

Cogs: S'a shammy.

Tam: Aye, it's a shammy – a 'c-h-a-m-o-i-s' (spells it) – O-I-S at the end. Comes from a French animal called a chamois. An' ye' only get

six cloths fae the wan animal – eight if it's a big yin.
Tam continued at the top of his voice.

Tam: Dae ye's hear me? They're no' fuckin' ten a penny. An' somebody's done this. Cogs, how dae ye' spall chamois?

Cogs: Dunno'.

Trish: It's C-H-A-M-O-I-S.

Tam: Aye that's right. See Cogs, ye' need a wee lassie tae tell ye' how
tae spell it.

All of these things, Tam's temper, his unpredictable nature, his sense of
humour, meant that boys' days were spent tinged with a certain amount of
fear and anxiety. They were aware of Tam's every move. Continually they
tried to work out when he would turn up, how he would react. They
misbehaved in ways which would least incur his wrath. He, on the other
hand, continually looked for new ways to catch boys out.

PUNISHMENT EXERCISES

To outsiders, boys in the paintshop could easily be seen to be equally
gainfully employed. In fact, the nature of tasks was very graded. Some
tasks were punitive and existed almost as a form of direct sanction.

Tam: Right you lassies, for the first few weeks ye's 'll no' get near a
paintbrush, ye'll jist be cleanin' up. Then we'll see how ye's shape up.
Ah'm pitten' ye's oan cleanin' door handles. A few days oan that an'
ah'll bet ye' never get paint oan another door handle.

We spent our first day with steel wool and scrapers, removing the paint
from hundreds of door handles. We worked furiously, trying to impress
Tam in the hope we would be allowed to stay. By the end of the day we had
finished. We sought out Tam and told him the good news – without the
desired effect. In fact, quite the opposite. Tam seemed positively put out.
The problem for him was that now it was up to him to generate more work
and that was a chore. Armed with cloths and pails we spent day two
cleaning two hundred or so windows. This job we tackled with a lot less
enthusiasm. In a short space of time we had learned an important lesson.
Apart from the real skills we were learning, we were also recognising that
being good workers entailed the ability to look busy, keep out of the way
and behave.

Davy and Nits started in the workshop two weeks after we did. They
learned the same lesson and just as quickly. Their first two days were spent
scraping paint off windows. They worked avidly with the same disap-
pointing results.

Nits: We've finished the windaes.

Tam: Ye've finished the windaes? Let's huv' a look. Whit's this?

Nits: Bit o' paint.

Tam: Ah thought ye' said ye'd finished.

They spent the next two days redoing it.

Tam subjectively assessed that some people need more of this kind of treatment than others.

Mo: That new guy [McVee] looks far too much like Spikey. He'll never get stayin'.

Spikey was an ex-trainee with a legendary reputation. He had defied Tam. Spikey had lasted a few short months. Like Spikey, McVee never managed to win Tam's confidence and never got beyond doing tasks which were punitive.

Davy was different. From one of the better housing estates, he looked older than his years, seemed mature, was neat and well dressed. He was earmarked from the start as a 'good painter'.

Frankie: That bastard Davy's gaunnae be wallpaperin' in a week – bet ye'.

Davy was painting alongside the other boys in two days.

Punishment exercises, then, were a feature of life for trainees and not only at the beginning of their time in the workshop. Jobs that were not jobs (but were punitive) were used to control and reassert control over boys throughout the year. Sweeping balconies was a classic task of this nature. To outsiders, boys sweeping up seem to be engaged in productive enough work. To a painter, a boy sweeping balconies meant one of two things. Either, boys who were doing it were new,

Nits: We've swept the balconies Tam.

Tam: We've swept them son? Well, whit's this?

Nits: Bit o' dust.

Tam: Dae it again son, eh?

or else it meant that boys had misbehaved. Sweeping up was a punishment task and a task without an end. The object for experienced boys was to look busy and to keep out of the way until Tam cooled down and decided it was time to rejoin the others. It was a boring task and mindless, and the amount of time spent sweeping up was directly linked to the severity of the misdemeanour.

'Picking flowers' was a similar job. Not the idyllic task the name suggests, the 'garden' was an overrun patch of ground at the side of the workshop. Being sent to work there was the severest of punishments. Tam caught Cogs and Pete, Craigie and Nits skiving. Rather than suspend them (his other option) he sent them to the 'garden'. Their brief was to pull up all the purple flowers (rosebay willowherb). Craigie and Nits, being new, set to the task with a vengeance. Impressively, several hours later, the monumental task was complete and they set out to tell Tam. The story is a familiar one.

Craigie: We've picked the purple flowers Tam.

Tam: Ye've picked them. Huv' ye' picked the yella' yins [dandelions]?

They set about this with a little less enthusiasm. But several hours later they reported to Tam again.

Craigie: That's the yella' yins Tam.

Tam: Well done boys. But there's plenty of dockins still to be picked. Then there's a' the green stuff [grass].

They rejoined Cogs and Pete and followed *their* example. They looked busy when it was appropriate, for the rest of the time they hung about bantering and chattering. They stayed there until Tam remembered about them and found them work. Some boys spent up to a week at a time in the garden. They looked productive, but achieved absolutely nothing.

It is difficult to think about discipline in the paintshop without thinking about analogies with the army. Order was kept in a regime partly based on fear. Parallels began on day one when new recruits received the harshest of treatment. Initially they were made to perform a series of boring, endless and meaningless tasks. This served several purposes. Tam asserted himself in control from the beginning. Respect for his anger and his discipline started early. His reasoning was that if you survived the first few weeks, you survived the course. It also ensured that after the first few awful weeks, when Tam eased off and when there was access to interesting work, trainees felt they were achieving something. They felt lucky and privileged. The tactic (usually) ensured their integration. It was justified at managerial level like this.

Jan: (training officer): Tam likes to make sure that new people are really keen.

Yet all of this had a slightly counter-intuitive outcome. Far from discouraging boys and destroying their faith in the workshop, boys in their own inimitable way actually respected Tam and what he was doing.

Frankie: Ah like Seafield. Ah've learnt a lot fae Tam. He's really, really scarey when he's mad. An' sometimes ah think he'll land somebody wan o' these days. Bit, if ye' dae ye'r work, he's fair. Tam's a' right. He makes ye' feel like ye're no' jist pissin' aboot. It's real.

Me: How d'ye like Tam?

Pete: He's an auld cunt.

Me: D'ye no' like him then?

Pete: Och, Tam's a'right. It's best fur yersel' when they're like that. Helps ye' get joabs.

THE GENERAL ATMOSPHERE

If the boys liked but felt ambiguously about Tam, they also felt the same about the nature of their 'jobs' in the paintshop.

Frankie: Och, Seafield widnae be a bad job if it wisnae fur the money. The work's a' right, an' ye' get no' bad holidays. Money's rubbish though.

Pete: Ah like it here. Ah'm learnin' 'hings. If ye' did 'hings wrong in other places they'd jist patch it up fur ye', as if ye' wir daft, didnae really matter. Ah'd rather hae a bollockin' fae Tam than that.

To understand boys' relationship to Tam, their attitude to work, we have to unfold the story a little further.

The general atmosphere of the paintshop itself felt like (and was set up to feel like) real work. Down to the smallest detail, the paintshop was supposed to resemble a real workplace. The organisation of discipline in Seafield generally, clocking in an out, the hooter marking the beginning and end of breaks, the formal warning system, all fed into and complemented what had been created in the paintshop. Boys accepted this. And inside the paintshop the resemblance to real work was even more pronounced. In the morning boys bantered around outside the paintshop until Tam or Robbie arrived to open up. This was a meaningful part of the day for boys. They had an image of men at work doing this and it pleased them to be able to do the same. They discussed and analysed what they had done the night before, who went out with whom, what they did, whether or not they had got drunk. The banter continued as they struggled into overalls and while Tam doled out the jobs for the day. They were real men about to embark on work for the day. They were serious and workmanlike.

'Pieces' are highly fetishised in most male workplaces and Seafield was no exception.

'Whit's yer ma' gien' ye' fur yer piece?'

'S' fuckin' cheese again'.

'Smarties, ah'll swop ye' an' egg piece fur wan oan ham.'

'Anybody goat ony sugar, ma fuckin' ma's forgot tae pit ony in.'

Painters ate their 'pieces' in a part of the building that was disused (the canteen). It felt for all the world like 'the hut' on a building site. There was a kettle, various assorted dirty cups. Tea was brewed, 'pieces' eaten and endlessly discussed. There was a large bench around which boys sat. It was more of a caricature of a real workplace than a workplace itself. Ten small men, manly in painters' overalls, simultaneously lit up ten cigarettes and picked up ten hands of cards. Painters particularly enjoyed leaving the workshop at lunchtime. They like to be seen in the street in their overalls as they went to buy cigarettes. All of these things allowed them to feel defined as manual workers with real jobs.

I want to move on now to discuss the more formal aspects of the work boys were offered in the paintshop. The main division was between what boys did when they were in the workshop and what they did when they were out on jobs.

JOBS OUT

Boys were regularly sent out to decorate churches, halls, community centres, old people's homes and houses, and to do other bits and pieces of decorating work. Jobs like these were commonly generated through supervisors' direct links with friends and trade friends outside the workshop. This is obviously a far cry from a commercial firm giving estimates, tendering for contracts, real wages and contracts. Yet Tam always discussed jobs for trainees in these latter terms, making an important issue out of 'doing his estimates', 'invoicing' people and finding contracts. For Tam, this provided him with an image of himself that he liked, buzzing around town in the van finding jobs for boys to do, costing them and providing estimates, and boys responded to this definition of work. 'Jobs out' were a central aspect of life for boys in the paintshop. They represented the most prestigious element of work there and the part of the job they most enjoyed.

The painters were the envy of the workshop. They had priority use of the van and impressed everyone as they loaded up (brushes, paint, scaffolding, kettles). Dressed in overalls, they piled into the van and drove off. 'Jobs out' represented the top of the jobs hierarchy to be striven and competed for:

> *Tam*: Right lads, there's a job oan at L.... Cogs, Pete, Punk Pete, Davy, Mo, in the van.

Boys who were seen to be good enough were allowed to do them. Everyone waited with baited breath to see whom Tam would choose, desperate to be included in the new job and out of the workshop for a long spell. The rest were left behind, despondent, to serve a 'pre-apprenticeship' (so to speak) in the workshop.

For boys who were chosen it meant the use of the best equipment in the workshop. On arrival at a new job, the van would be quickly and efficiently unloaded.

> *Tam*: Right you laddies, Cogs and Mo strip a' the wa's. Loads o' water, right. Sand them doon a bit first. When that's done – these wa's arnae even – so we're gaunnae put up linin' paper. How'd ye' pit up linin' paper Cogs?
>
> *Cogs*: Roon' the wa', no' up an' doon.
>
> *Tam*: Right, get started.

Tam would typically leave, going back to the workshop to check on the other boys. Boys on this job worked unsupervised. They did it in a mature and hardworking way and in a way which impressed everyone who passed by. The first task was always to find an appropriate place, away from the public eye, to have lunch. (On this particular job it was a small basement underneath the stair.) Here boys relaxed – off stage. They sat around joking, chatting, eating and swopping 'pieces', drinking lemonade and playing tapes. This was one of the highlights of being out on a job, a time when they particularly felt that this is what real work would be like.

PERKS

Like workers anywhere, boys lived for perks. Here boys were grateful for very little. Tam allowed boys an hour for lunch (rather than half an hour) when they were out on jobs. It was justified in terms of real men at work.

> *Tam* Ye get an hour for lunch when ye're oot. It'd be like that if ye' were workin'. It's mair flexible.

Sometimes the small perks they received (and for which they were so grateful) were sad and particularly touching. Traditionally workers leave work early on a Friday to go to the pub. *In* the workshop, boys were never allowed away early. Out on jobs though (as in real jobs) Tam often let boys away slightly before time. Under age for the pub, they had created their own substitute. Driving back to town, the van would commonly be stopped outside a baker's shop. Seven or eight boys would celebrate the end of the week by devouring synthetic cream cakes which must have been all of a foot long.

JOBS IN

Although 'jobs out' were central, in fact trainees spent a large part of their time inside the workshop. Trainees did 'jobs in' during the long weeks when Tam was unable to generate sufficient numbers of 'jobs out' to keep boys occupied.

Inside the workshop, boys learned in an informal way. Typically, Tam would demonstrate a new task once. After that, boys were on their own, learning directly or by watching others. Improvement came with repetition and practice, direct instruction from Tam being rare.

At an earlier stage in the development of Seafield as a workshop, activities took on a more meaningful form. When the building first became available, large parts were derelict. Professional tradesmen did the bulk of the renovation, but supervisors and groups of boys did a significant amount of work as well. However, once this was completed, work in the paintshop involved little more than continually decorating and redecorating the same parts of the building (for practice). The canteen had been painted twice in the time I was there and windows in the joinery shop were painted by each successive group of YOPs.

Trainees were well aware that the work they did inside the workshop was largely about filling up time. For boys to be in the workshop was second best. For weeks on end they were stuck there with little to do apart from the small jobs that Tam managed to generate. No-one liked these times. An atmosphere hung over the workshop when 'jobs out' were scarce, an atmosphere of waiting, hoping that something outside would turn up. Yet the irony of all this was perhaps that boys found this as valid and acceptable a part of life in the workshop as 'jobs out'; they were almost as well behaved inside the workshop as they were out. For Tam (as well as for boys) the definitive training experience was outside (jobs out). For supervisors, being around the workshop without work was as demoralising an experience as it was for boys. Tam could never raise any enthusiasm for hanging superfluous doors from walls to demonstrate to boys how to paint them. Apprentices do not learn like this and neither would boys in Seafield. Boys took on board what Tam assumed to be important aspects of work and shared them. For boys, being 'out' was real work, and provided them (and Tam) with their reason to be in the workshop. At separate times both Tam and Charlie explained to me how bored they got inside the workshop. After a lifetime in the decorating trade, they found it claustrophobic. It was legitimated and made acceptable to boys thus: what happened in Seafield was no different from what happened in real workplaces. Decorating firms in the real world have slack periods. Workers hang around doing very little for weeks on end. This was Tam's explanation. Boys accepted it.

THE PACE OF WORK

Apart from the more formal aspects of 'work' in the paintshop, trainees were also initiated into other less formal aspects of work in the real world.

I talked in the section on 'punishment exercises' about how one could impress Tam. It was not working quickly and efficiently that was valued by Tam. In the paintshop it consistently fell back on him to generate more and more jobs. Part of the training in the paintshop involved learning to know which jobs were real jobs that had to be done quickly and efficiently, and which jobs were fillers. The best trainees were not the ones who completed jobs in record time, rather the best trainees knew how to pace work, when to complete a job when Tam wanted it completed. Looking busy and conscientious was more important than actually being busy. And boys who grasped the essence of this were the boys most favoured by Tam. This initiation into the more informal and hidden aspects of the world of work was as important a skill to learn as decorating.

When Trish started, she desperately wanted to be allowed to stay, to please Tam. She worked as fast and as well as possible. All she wanted was to go to Tam and say she had finished. She wanted him to say, 'That's wonderful, Trish, you did that in record time.' In fact, that was the last thing that Tam wanted. Finishing a job quickly simply meant he had to generate another – and there was a limit to the number of jobs he could create. What Tam wanted was to be able to go up quietly to a group of boys and to say: 'Wind that up you laddies. There's something else ah want ye's tae dae.' The important thing for him was not so much that everyone was working fast and well as that everyone was seen to be working fast and well. The workshop had its own pace. A job was given out for a day or for a morning, boys worked on it and Tam decided when it was time to stop. New people, unaware of the informal pace of work, inevitably threw a spanner into the works. They were resented.

The favoured boys looked busy and kept out of the way. Again (as in real work), no-one taught new boys informal rules (about the pace of work, about which jobs were fillers and which were punishment exercises). They learned the hard way and boys who picked this up slowly were scorned. Boys who never learned were universally ostracised as 'sooks', disliked by Tam as well.

Pete and Cogs were best. They were respected by the rest of the boys and by Tam. What Tam wanted they had down to a fine art. Sometimes it seemed they could almost read his mind. They paced work exactly, did enough to seem good, not enough to seem like 'sooks' or be bored. They made jobs spin out when times were slack and when Tam was short on ideas. They worked flat out when they had to. They were exceptionally skilled.

One Friday afternoon, we had finished the job we had been working on all week. A new job was to begin on Monday. We made the few cleaning up jobs that were left last for four hours. Most of the day was spent idly chatting, leaping to attention when anyone was heard approaching. An incomer would have entered a hive of productivity and industry.

This hidden, informal aspect of life in the paintshop was an important factor in making the workshop acceptable to boys. Their attempts to work out how to fit into this aspect of life in the paintshop, to establish the pace to work at – what different kinds of work meant – made boys feel that they were getting a taste of what life in a real workplace would be like and that they were engaged in a project that was challenging and interesting.

DISRUPTION IN THE PAINTSHOP

Limited resistance

Simply because boys appeared to be individually competitive and hard-working did not mean they were not disruptive. They were. But because what was offered them in the workshop was largely acceptable to them, the disruption was usually within well-defined limits.

> *Tam:* I heard a nasty rumour that some o' you laddies huv' been takin' long tea breaks. Ye's ken who ah mean (Shouting) Ye's ken who ah mean!
> *Chorus:* Aye.
> *Tam:* You guys get enough privileges – ah'm no' huvin' them abused. If ah hear wan mair rumour, ah swear tae god, ye's'll no' know whit's hit ye'.

Sometimes resistance took place simply because Tam allowed it to. It was an acceptable and allowable way for men at work to behave. Here it became something of a game – the limits and rules of which were set by Tam. For example, as a general rule, smoking was not allowed in workshops. Boys in the workshop were unofficially allowed to smoke, yet they never smoked when outsiders were around and stopped as soon as anyone came in. They smoked in contravention of general workshop rules, but within limits set by Tam. General carry-on around the workshop took the same form. Tam knew boys carried-on and were high spirited. As long as it stopped immediately Tam (or anyone else) entered the room this was acceptable. Tam was aware that work was slack, that often there was no real work to keep boys occupied. Boys were allowed to carry-on in these circumstances – so long as no-one knew about it. On entering a room Tam was often aware that a second beforehand boys had been skiving, but so long as the place looked like a hive of industry when he walked in he was satisfied.

Part of the richness of life in the paintshop centred around the relationship that Tam and the boys were locked into around the issue of limits and

acceptable behaviour. Tam set limits which were narrow. (Acceptable
levels of carry-on were set at the level of what would have been acceptable
at work.) And they relished the challenge of finding ways to resist that did
not incur the wrath of Tam.

Resistance in practice

Trish and I had been painting door frames for days. Most of the work
involved being outside. We were bored and cold. We went to the toilet –
more as a diversion and to heat up than anything else. Once there, we got
caught up in conversation with some of the girls from knitwear (also
passing time). We were probably away for about fifteen minutes. When we
got back Tam was leaning against our ladder waiting for us. This was a
major transgression. Trish and I were terrified, my knees were weak with
shock at having been caught out this way. Tam was pleased, I suspect, to
have caught us on the hop on this occasion and Trish and I got off lightly.

> *Tam*: Where huv' you' lassies been? Don't ever let me catch you's at
> that again.

As far as I at least was concerned, he never would.

On another occasion, Trish and I had been painting windows outside
the canteen. Again we were bored and cold. Our stuff for making tea lay
temptingly inside the doorway.

> *Trish*: Gaunnae nash in an' stick the kettle oan fur a cup o' tea. Ah'll
> keep shotty.

> *Me*: Whit! Are ye' daft? Tam'll make mincemeat oot o' us.

We debated it nervously, giggling uncontrollably at the thought. Eventually I went in and put on the kettle. My heart was thumping. I do not think
a single boy would have done this. With me now keeping shotty, Trish
went in and prepared two steaming cups of coffee and laid them and two
Kit Kats on the window ledge. At the same moment I saw Tam and Robbie
walk along the balcony towards us. I could not believe my eyes. I panicked,
but I did have the presence of mind (just) to rush in and warn Trish. With
more presence of mind than me, Trish dumped the cups underneath the
radiator and stood in front of them. I tried to paint.

> *Tam*: How's it goin' girls? That's the stuff.

For form's sake he took the brush out of my hand and in a token way
painted a bit of my door. He then walked off unconcerned. Unbelievably,
we had gotten away with it. As soon as he was out of sight we collapsed,
giggling and laughing hysterically. This went on all day.

> *Trish*: God, ye'd 'hink we'd robbed a bank or summat', no' fuckin'
> made a shitey wee cup o' tea.

Tormenting people

Disruption, insofar as it happened at all in the paintshop, was hidden. It
had to be able to be stopped quickly, it could not involve objects which
could easily be found. One of the most popular ways of misbehaving was

simply annoying people. This commonly started off verbally. It often
ended up far from verbal. This formed one part of boys' (small) hidden
culture from which Tam was excluded. It was one of their main tactics used
to avert boredom and get through the day. And once again, it seemed
(superficially) disruptive and challenging. In the long run, however, it
made the workshop a more exciting and acceptable place for boys.

A lot of boys' energy went into 'tormenting' people and into creating
situations to make this happen. Boys who were skilled at this had standing
and status among other boys (as well as, incidentally, with Tam). Tormenting people implied finding out enough about people to know what it was
they were sensitive about, then teasing them about it endlessly. Typically,
events proceeded like this.

Craigie: Frankie's burst his glue bag. He 'hinks ye' sook no' blaw.

Frankie worked hard and had a reputation for being a good painter. He
rarely carried on (even when the coast was completely clear). Other boys
spent a lot of time tormenting him. It generally centred around the fact that
Frankie boasted.

Me: How come ye's call Frankie, Gibber?

Mo: S'obvious. He gibbers a load o' shite. He's gaunnae be fightin' six
boys the morn single-handed.

Frankie: Shur' up.

Mo: Frankie, sure an' you beat up three boys last night?

Frankie: Shut it, ye'r really buggin' me.

Mo: Killed ony mair gorillas yet?

Frankie: Ye wantin' yer' fuckin' face kicked in?

Mo: Aye me an' three other boys an' all, an' you'll hae wan arm tied
behind yer' back.

Frankie, pushed to the limit, threw a huge piece of putty across the room.
It caught Mo on the right temple. Mo retaliated by throwing it back.
Everyone else ducked quickly down behind benches. Everyone picked up
putty and sawdust at that point (and anything else which could be
launched). A generalised battle started. Steven, the punk, moved outside
the door to keep shotty. One sign from him and the place was transformed
instantly into the tranquil, hard-working atmosphere of a model workshop.

The ridiculous to the sublime

Resistance, if limited in the paintshop, was at the same time incredibly
varied. It ranged from being crass, childish and individualistic, to being
collective, clever and well-thought-out. What was characteristic about all
of it was that it was hidden, separated off from Tam, at sharp odds with
how boys normally related to him. I will give two (polar) examples to
demonstrate.

Four or five of us were working together to finish a room. We did not
have much to do and Tam wanted to make it last until the end of the week.

We were bored. A couple of boys disappeared into a huge cupboard at the back of the room. For half an hour hysterical laughs and squeals emanated from the back of the room. I was curious and nervous about the kind of perverse practices that may have been going on there. Eventually I went to investigate. There were three boys so hysterical with laughter they were dripping with sweat. They emerged from the cupboard with red and swollen wrists. They had spent the entire time playing a game that involved smashing each other on the wrists with two fingers. They were greatly amused at their own daring.

> *Me*: God, you lot are murder.
> *Pete*: Aye, ah ken, this is whit this place drives ye' tae, playin' like the
> primary school.

This incident typified resistance in the workshop. It was hidden, it did not overtly disrupt the smooth-running of the workshop and at a second's warning it could quickly have been stopped.

The second example is more sophisticated. On a boy's first day in the paintshop he was given the necessary tools of the trade – ritually handed over into his personal care are a pair of overalls (to be carefully looked after and washed every second week) and a scraper. There was a heavy penalty to be paid for loss of a scraper. And boys (like real decorators) kept them in a special pocket in the leg of their overalls. Despite their preciousness, scrapers invariably went missing. And at any given time there were fewer scrapers than boys. The 'game' involved every boy making sure that he always had a scraper. If you had one you guarded it. If not, you would try to find one – if someone was silly enough to leave one lying around, you picked it up and pocketed it. Or worse, you stole one out of someone else's pocket. This was one aspect of the game. The other was supportive and collective.

> *Tam*: Where's yer' scraper sonny?
> *Mo*: S'upstairs.
> *Tam*: Well dinnae leave it lyin' aboot, eh! Go an' get it.

Mo went upstairs and Cogs gave him his.

> *Tam*: Where's yer' scraper?
> *Pete*: Frankie's got it.

Frankie handed his over to Pete. And so it went on. This was, in a sense, the pinnacle of boys' disruption in the paintshop. It was in many ways a classic example of workplace resistance – cleverly and collectively worked out. Yet in this context it demonstrated as much as anything why boys were integrated. It was not only the more formal aspects of work in the paintshop which boys enjoyed and which were acceptable, it was the complete culture. And this informal aspect of life integrated them as much as anything. It gave them the sense of identity they wanted, defined them as meaningfully and gainfully employed and provided them with a daily experience that was never boring. And, incidentally, it was the smartest boys (in Tam's terms) who were also best at indulging in their own culture, doing it in such a way that meant they would never be caught. Wildly hurling putty one minute, work was always to hand at a second's notice, and the next moment they could look as if they had been diligently working for the whole of the morning. Any situation could lend itself to 'tormenting' and being 'tormented'. Walking past scaffolding, someone would would drop a dust sheet on you, Tam would walk in and the scene could be transformed into one of folding it up. Walking past a ladder, someone would leap on you, near a sink and someone would slosh you with paint. Putty fights continued off and on for days. All these things were instantly transformed into scenes of industry.

The daily culture of the paintshop then was an interesting and highly energetic one. Boys worked hard in a formal sense. They also put a lot into generating a lively and complicated culture of their own – a form of limited resistance, largely separated off from official sources (though at the same time defined by them) and hidden. It was subtle, not directly confrontational with supervisors, and always carried out with one eye on being discovered. They had an ability to freeze and transform a situation of chaos into a scene of productivity. They did it with impressive ease. Boys' creativeness and energy in this area was concerned with working (and not working) within acceptable limits. And far from ultimately challenging the status quo, in this context, boys' resistance had the effect of creating a total cultural context which reinforced the paintshop as a place where boys wanted to be.

I want to look now at what happens to boys in the admittedly rare instances when what is offered is not acceptable. I want to do this using the example of one boy. It is interesting in its own right, but also provides further insights and evidence into what it was about the paintshop that made it acceptable to the majority of boys.

MCVEE: A CASE OF REJECTION

I have already described the process through which trainees were carefully screened at Seafield. Potentially disruptive young people were selected out at the interview stage. (Driven by 'market forces', there is no commitment to taking problem trainees with a view to integrating them.) In Seafield everyone had to pull their weight. Trainees who did not come over as hard-working and keen at interview stood little chance of being accepted. Potential discipline problems were already minimised by this process.

> *Jan*: We only take those we think we can help. If it's obvious they're not going to be keen, then we don't bother.

> *Tam*: We're here tae gie these laddies a trade, we're no' bloody social workers. We're no' wanting anybody who's no' interested in daein' a hard day's work. Robbie an' me dae a good day's work. We're no' carryin' anybody.

A few though did slip through the net. McVee was one. I learned a lot about Seafield through McVee. More than any other boy, McVee pushed Tam's definitions to the limit. Indeed, it was through McVee that I first came to understand the full extent to which boys were integrated and accepting.

In order to understand what he brought to the workshop, the attitude to work that he had, it is important to say a little bit about his life outside. McVee was a 'skin'. Previously he had hung around on the streets in a gang. He had created for himself a supportive network and a significant culture that was not reliant on school. He had set up a structure and meaning to his life on the dole. I am not arguing here that McVee enjoyed being on the dole. He did not. He hated it. But what made him different from other boys was that for him (in contrast to them), a return to the dole was thinkable. It was a realistic, if depressing option. Unlike other boys, who latched on to Seafield, McVee had an identity that was not formed instantly on arrival. He had an identity outside, a life to return to and good friends. Six of his friends accompanied him as far as the gate on his first day. All day they popped their heads up and down over the wall, grinning and laughing at McVee and at each other. Each day after that several boys were always to be found, half an hour before the hooter, hanging around waiting to walk McVee home. This went down very badly with staff.

McVee had utter contempt for schemes like this. Had 'careers' not sent him, he would never have come. He had no intention of liking it or trying it and no intention of staying. From the beginning he leapt around wildly, cursing, swearing, bantering around. The rest of the boys were amused and by four o'clock they were laying bets:

Cogs: Ah'll gie him tae the end o' the week.

Pete: That man'll no' last tae the morra'.

McVee's energy was impressive. He talked non-stop, bawled, shouted, one minute lying flat on his back on the floor, the next, leaping on top of a cupboard nine feet high, from there on to a ladder, off that and on to a bench. Then he would run around on top of every bench in the place. As yet (more by luck than good judgement) he did this when supervisors were out. He took few precautions against being caught, and it seemed only a matter of time before he seriously contravened the rules.

Other boys' reactions to McVee were telling. They generally liked him and enjoyed his patter. They found him immensely entertaining. But they (like me) enjoyed him as a misfit, an aberration that was temporary. They observed him with ironic amusement, interested, more than anything, in how long he would last. But they kept their distance. No-one wanted to be tarred with the same brush as McVee. They encouraged him from a distance, as the best diversion from the boredom that had happened in a long while. His behaviour and fate were the central talking point around the workshop for weeks.

McVee: Haw, heid the ba', 'hink ah kin hing upside doon by ma feet fae this ladder?

Pete: Heid the ba'. The cunt's crazy.

Unbelievably, McVee did last a week. And even more unbelievably perhaps, his behaviour slowly began to change. It was a subtle and imperceptible change, invisible to the untrained eye. As he weighed up what was happening in the paintshop, he modified his ideas and he changed his mind. Slowly he warmed to the idea of Seafield as an alternative to the dole. He was seduced by the same thing that seduced all the boys. The idea of being a real painter with a real job began to seem real and appealing.

McVee was not allowed a paintbrush to himself. He had, though, spent enough time in rooms with boys who were painting to appreciate how much they liked it. He began to want the same.

McVee: Gie's a shot o' that, Mo.

In the absence of Tam, Mo would hand over the paintbrush and McVee would be quiet for ages, concentrating, painting and getting it right.

McVee: How dae ye' dae this again, Mo? Whit dae ye' use this brush fur?

He was still 'crazy', but slowly he became different. Like the rest, he was tempted by the idea of what it would feel like to wear overalls, to paint and to be allowed out on jobs. McVee had rejected a long time ago the idea of ever finding work, but here it began to seem almost possible. He began to care, to want to stay. He still carried on, but began to keep one eye on the door. We all noticed the change. Our new preoccupation was with whether or not it was to late.

That McVee came to hold a new attitude was surprising. Given the exceptionally (even for Tam) harsh treatment he received from Tam it was even more surprising. All new boys received a harsh initiation as a matter of course. From the outset it was obvious to Tam that McVee was unsuitable, that he had slipped through a net. Subsequently he met with even harsher treatment than most. In all the time in the workshop, McVee was not given one decent job. The content of all his days were singularly boring, punitive and meaningless. He swept balconies for his first week, for the second he weeded the garden. Other boys mostly never commented on such things. They did in McVee's case.

Cogs: S'no' fair, nae other guy has ever hud tae spend a whole week in the gairden. Tam's really oot tae get him.

MCVEE'S DEMISE

The build-up to McVee's demise actually turned out to be a fairly protracted affair. McVee had been given his first painting job. It was late Friday afternoon. Trish, McVee, Craigie, Nits and I had been standing on separate window sills in the joiners' shop painting windows all day. We were exhausted, bored and desperate to get home.

Without McVee, the time would have gone much more slowly. He had entertained us all day, jumping around and keeping up a constant stream of patter. He did this in a much more restrained way though, partly due to the fact that he was so pleased with himself because Tam had found him overalls and given him a paintbrush. He had also been taught how to paint a window frame. It was his first taste of the good life, of the things that the rest of the boys were taking for granted. And in between joking around, he worked hard. He had actually been working quietly and carefully for a long time when disaster struck. He accidently stepped back and kicked his whole pot of paint off the window ledge. There was a deathly pause and we all looked at each other in horror. Our hearts sank. McVee had committed a cardinal sin – paintpots had to be held, never, never laid down where they could be kicked over. An image of Tam and what his reaction would be passed through all our minds. We stared at each other, then, as one, we leapt on the paint, scooping it into our own pots with scrapers, wiping it up with anything to hand – rags, paper, sticks.

Tam appeared at the other end of the workshop ten seconds too soon. The first thing he saw was paint running down the side of McVee's tin on to the floor. He rushed over and grabbed the brush and pot from McVee, angry enough to burst.

Tam: That laddie's no' fit tae hae a paintbrush in his hand.

It was then he noticed the huge glob of paint on the window ledge. He stood speechless with rage for all of ten seconds, growing redder and redder. Then he let loose at McVee. He yelled and roared at McVee. I was terrified. McVee was kept back after four and Tam gave him more of the same. I spent the weekend thinking McVee would be fired. Tam had wanted that. The workshop hierarchy insisted that (in accordance with rules) McVee be given a written warning. And now, Tam was really out to get him.

Unfortunately for McVee, one of the consequences of his presence in the workshop meant that space had been made for other people to misbehave without blame. The other boys had a scapegoat and used McVee to the full. During that week, there was an upsurge of graffiti. Some of it was certainly McVee, some of it I know was not. It was not McVee who wrote 'Tam's an auld cunt' on the paintshop wall. McVee was blamed anyway.

McVee may or may not have survived in the workshop, but on top of all of this he committed the ultimate sin. What eventually finished McVee was (significantly) not something that took place inside the workshop, but outside. Like in public schools, Seafield boys have to be Seafield boys inside as well as out. Outside (it was said), they carried the whole reputation of the workshop. On one occasion an instructor from an outdoor centre took a group of boys canoeing. Free from the discipline of the workshop, faced with a liberal teacher and the great outdoors, plus McVee's encouragement, they all went mad. They deliberately capsized canoes, told the guy to 'fuck off' and somehow intimidated him into driving them home to their individual houses. They topped everything by leaving the van in an unbelievable mess. In the workshop behaviour like this was bad enough. Outside, it reflected on the supervisor, on this occasion Tam, and he took it as a personal insult. Boys had never acted this badly before. The only factor that was different was McVee and McVee was duly blamed for committing the worst crime it was possible to commit. He was called into the office, verbally abused and sacked and he left the workshop in tears. That he had altered all the fire notices in the place before he went was the sting in the tail that was not noticed until later.

In Event of Fire
1. Throw Tam in.
2. Pick up two big tins of gloss paint and run.
3. Assemble at Robbie's house for tea and biscuits.

For most of the boys who ended up in the paintshop, their experience of school had been mixed. On the positive side, they had friends and an institutional setting from which to relate to them. For most of them, the experience of unemployment had cut this off sharply. They had come to the workshop from a situation of isolation and with very few friends left that they saw regularly. By the time they were interviewed at the workshop, most were open to giving the workshop a chance. McVee was different. And boys who had a structure to their lives, an identity and friends outside the workshop, had a different basis upon which to assess the workshop.

JOBS FOR THE BOYS: REFERENCES, QUALIFICATIONS AND APPRENTICESHIPS

The paintshop had one more thing to offer boys which ensured their acceptance.

> *Robbie*: OK you guys, o'er here, ah want tae talk tae ye's. Ah've jist heard that Keith (ex-trainee) has been taken can wi' D… (local decorating firm). He wiz started intae the second year o' his apprenticeship – no' the first year – dae ye's hear – the second year. An' ah jist want tae try an' impress wan thing oan you guys, the reason Keith got tae'n oan wi' D…wiz because o' his reference. Noo, ah jist hope you guys are listenin', especially some o' you guys who are aboot half way through – it pays tae muck in – ah'm tellin' ye's.

If the content of work and the fact that the way skills were passed on was culturally relevant to boys and was an important factor in winning their approval of the scheme, then the promise and the hope of jobs to go on to at the end was an important part of this. It was the carrot held out to trainees from the beginning. The reputation of Seafield was partly built on its good record of placing trainees in jobs. And the good behaviour of boys, the acceptance of somewhat authoritarian discipline was bought partly on the basis of this promise. Boys and supervisors talked continually about references. And in contrast to school, they recognised the importance of getting good references. When boys were sanctioned, it was often the first thing they mentioned.

Sharkey had been in the 'garden' for four days. He had been caught 'skiving'. He was subdued when he rejoined the rest of the group

> *Sharkey*: Ah may as well jist go hame. Ah'll never get a good reference noo.

Trainees were assessed monthly and were well aware that how they performed would be reflected in the reference they would eventually get. The build-up to it revealed a lot.

At the end of the month, supervisors filled in an assessment sheet for every trainee. Trainees were called into the office individually. In the presence of their supervisor and the training officer, their progress was gone over verbally. On the surface boys took it lightly. They joked, poured scorn on the event, but were nervous and affected by it all the same. On the day, trainees lined up outside the office. They questioned each other carefully on the way out.

Cogs: Whit'd he say aboot you?

Frankie: He says ah've goat leadership qualities. He kin leave me in a room wi' two or three new guys an' ah ken whit's whit. Says ma punctuality's a bit doon though.

Wee Rab: He says ah'm a great worker, sometimes, inconsistent but...

Pete: He says ah wiz good oan everythin'.

Cogs: Bet Stafford's is glowin', Stafford's a sook.

At the time of the study a significant number of boys *did* move on to apprenticeships with local firms. Jobs, though, were not set up out of the new vocationalism, out of arrangements set up by the MSC, nor were they set up through the training officer in the office, or the careers service. Seafield's reputation for placing trainees in jobs hinged on more informal arrangements than that. It was built on the contacts and knowledge working-class supervisors had with the local labour market. Boys too were more familiar with local job possibilities than were the office staff, and they were familiar with the workings of local decorating firms. They knew them by name, were aware of the number of apprentices they had and the times of year they took them on. Their knowledge was partly picked up outside the workshop from friends and relatives. It was added to by Tam.

When a 'good boy' neared the end of his year in the paintshop, typically Tam or Robbie started asking round. They kept their eyes and ears open. Personal contacts from the past ensured they heard of vacancies as soon as anyone did. Indeed, a big part of their job identity depended on their ability to place boys.

Robbie: (about an exceptionally good boy):

Ah'll get that laddie a place if ah've tae get in the van masel' an' take him roon every firm in toon.

Thus, the commonplace assumption that young people in Seafield got jobs because of its good reputation, that trainees were well-disciplined and received a good training, were unfounded. Trainees got jobs because working-class tradesmen were well placed to get them for them. The significant thing about boys' behaviour was that the jobs that supervisors generated were partly used to enforce a standard of work and good behaviour from boys; the boys were required to compete with each other for the jobs available. Presumably even if Tam and Robbie did not work there, they (and others like them) would/could use their contacts to find work for other boys (relatives of young people or young people living near by). The informal ways in which older men and younger boys knew about the local job market was harnessed here, and around it was built a whole new way of organising young people. What could be an informal arrangement for ensuring that some young people get access to the very few jobs that exist has become, for Tam, his work, and forms the basis of a whole new way of defining and thinking about young people.

TO CONCLUDE

To an outsider, the image of Seafield is the image of the office. The office was tastefully and well decorated (cream paintwork, brown carpet, plants). In every respect it could have been the administrative centre of any commercial office. The professional image was reinforced by management personnel themselves. All of them were young and middle-class. And it was partly in relation to this that the MSC interpreted Seafield as a model scheme. The reality of the reputation, though, lay somewhere different, and was often at complete odds with the image of Seafield that management was trying to build.

In sharp contrast to the office, male supervisors were tradesmen and working-class. They were without training or sophistication and without qualifications. They were rough, ready and unpolished, hired on the basis of trade skills. And boys' acceptance of Seafield was on the basis of what they created for themselves and for trainees. The atmosphere was one which boys felt close to culturally and could understand. Boys were learning skills that were culturally relevant to them in a setting that was acceptable. Real jobs as painters and decorators were what boys most wanted in the world. In the absence of this, a close approximation to it was set up in Seafield. It provided them with the opportunity to build an image of themselves as real men with real jobs. For all of the reasons I have discussed – the nature of work in the paintshop, the offer and hope of jobs at the end, the complete absence of anything positive in their lives as an alternative – meant that few boys were ever in a position to do anything other than to grasp wholeheartedly what was on offer in the paintshop and they rarely challenged workshop discipline in a way that was directly threatening to order there.

3
JOINERS

In this chapter I want to compare joiners with painters. I want to look at how similar boys with similar expectations and attitudes arbitrarily allocated to one workshop or the other, experienced and reacted to Seafield in different ways. The main difference between painters and joiners is best revealed in the following.

THE FOOTBALL MATCH

Occasionally in the workshop a football match was organised between painters and joiners. Everyone piled into the minibus and drove to the local playing fields. Excitement was high. It was an afternoon without work and with full pay. The joiners' enjoyment of the trip was different from the painters. They made the most of the trip, joking, fighting, laying bets on the score, eating rubbish, drinking fizzy juice. By contrast, the painters sat still, grim-faced and serious. They were out to win.

At the football ground Frankie (the best painter) had already set himself up as leader, and he was angry. Predictably, the two punks in the group (Punk Pete and Steven) and Elvis (the Elvis Presley look-alike) refused to play. Playing football was not an image any of them wanted to project. Frankie was outraged at their lack of commitment. Besides, without their presence on the field the painters were forced to play with ten men. By contrast, the joiners lay around the grass bantering, making small talk with supervisors. Supervisors had trouble persuading *any* of them to play.

Joe (supervisor):

Come oan you lads, they're oot there in a circle talkin' tactics. They're gaunnae run rings roon' ye's. Ye's'll need tae pull yersel's the gither boys. Come oan, ye've been training fur this fur three weeks. Ah'm ah gaun' tae huv' tae play masel'?

Half way through the match, despite the singlemindedness of their approach, the painters were in trouble. Most serious was the problem of the goalkeeper's boots. They nipped his feet and he was in agony. A substitute was desperately needed. Frankie scowled at the sidelines. The three substitutes sat tight. Elvis was the first to break. Fear of future retribution overcame his sense of protectiveness for his image. And hurling abuse over his shoulder at the punks, he took his place in the goalmouth.

Elvis: Ya lazy, shitey bastards, ah'll get ye's fur this.

In fact Elvis need not have worried. He managed to maintain his Presley image intact even under these circumstance. To the fury of his teammates, Elvis's attempts to retrieve the ball were far from vigorous. At most he would shuffle towards a low ball, hands in pockets, hips thrust out, flick back his hair and deflect the ball with his foot. All this to roars of 'dive Elvis, fuckin' dive'. Despite two glorious goals scored by Frankie and Pete (the blue-eyed boys of the paintshop), despite the joiners' giggling and laughing throughout the second half of the game, the painters lost. The goalkeeper had lost the game for the painters and would never be forgiven. Chavvy (one of the joiners) summed up the painters' efforts:

Chavvie: Did ye' see Frankie Gibber? Nearly burst his heart gettin' the ba' past me. Ver' near hacked aff ma' legs. The painters ur' a' sooks.

The same attitudes were reflected by the two groups in their approaches to work. One explanation for this was that different workshops had different recruitment patterns. Painters were taken on one by one throughout the year. They started into a structure that was ongoing and already established. Individually they had to find their own way of fitting in. This created an atmosphere of rivalry, hierarchy and a sense of competition among painters. Joiners, on the other hand, began their year together as a group. As a result they were more cohesive. They set themselves up in opposition to supervisors. Undoubtedly this was one important factor in explaining the difference between painters and joiners. It was not the only one.

Like the paintshop, the joinery shop housed fifteen boys and there were two supervisors (Joe and Neil). Again, supervisors were working-class and tradesmen. This workshop too felt like a workplace – male, stark and (to me) unwelcoming. In this case it was a long room. One end was filled with work benches, chairs and lockers. Boys left 'pieces' and belongings here. It was where boys spent most of their time, surrounded by mountains of wood, saws, hammers, putty, nails and sawdust. The back of the workshop was the machine room. There was cutting machinery, ancient and variously acquired.

Unlike the paintshop, however, the image of 'model trainees' was not one which could easily be applied to joiners. The good reputation of Seafield was not founded here. Joiners had a reputation for being noisy, boisterous and irresponsible. In comparison with painters, they were seen as second-rate, less workmanlike, immature and lazy. This attitude was shared by trainees, management and supervisors.

Fran: Whit did ye' 'hink o' the joiners?

Me: A' right. A bit borin'.

Fran: The joiners are horrible, they're dead babyish.
Cath: Sometimes ah wonder whit Joe and Neil are up tae doon there. Tha' laddies get away wi' murder.

From the vantage point of the paintshop this was the image of them I had. Where painters' disruption was hidden and contained, joiners carried-on in places that were public. Their noisiness and boisterousness annoyed. To understand this we need to begin by looking at supervisors.

JOE

Joe and Tam were similar in many ways. Joe too was working-class and a tradesman – he had spent most of his working life as a site joiner. When the job at Seafield came up he was only too pleased to have lighter work.

> *Joe:* Ah used tae go here there and everywhere lookin' fur the big money, leavin' ma wife tae bring up the six weans hursel'. It wiz really cut throat – ah'm tellin' ye. Ah'm really glad tae be oot o' it noo. This is a much easier job.

Like Tam, the way Joe structured boys' days and what he thought of as important and meaningful in terms of work came out of his own needs in terms of his own job satisfaction. In so far as boys in the joinery shop were well behaved, they were well behaved for the same reasons as painters. That they were more disruptive was because certain things were simply less achievable in the joinery shop. Indeed, it is tempting to attribute the differences in the workshop to the differences in the personalities of the two men. For all their similarities, Tam and Joe were very different. In the paintshop boys behaved partly because Tam was tough and authoritarian. Joe was lenient and boys misbehaved.

Tam and Joe had different ideas about trainees and indeed about the nature of YOP. Joe's attitudes were partly wrought out of his disillusionment with his own attempts to change things. He grasped the aims and ideals of Seafield less wholeheartedly than Tam. His response to the workshop had varied over time. When he first took the job he had been enthusiastic.

> *Joe:* Meetin' after meetin' ah've stood up an' said, 'it's a bloody disgrace'. A couple o' times Cath [supervisor in knitwear] had dragged me tae meetin's aboot it – gettin' them mair pay, gettin' them intae unions – an' ah'm a' fur it. But ah've a' ended up embarrassed at the meetin's. They've always turned oot tae be political sorts o' things. Cath's a bit like that. Ah'm a bit o' a socialist masel; but ye' get fed up wi' it after a while – ah dinnae go tae meetin's noo. An' we're no' bloody social workers. We're jist here tae gie them a good trainin' – it's a' ye' can dae.

For Joe, working at Seafield was fraught with contradictions. Personally, he liked the job and was glad to be out of the building trade. But he was aware that the job involved imposing on trainees something that was unfair.

> *Joe:* Ah couldnae push them hard, no' fur £23. It's a bloody disgrace.

Joe, though, was now disillusioned. He put very little into the job. All too often he would be found at the back of the workshop with the machines. The products of these hours were impressive – exquisitely made boxes of different kinds of wood, inlaid and ornate. For Joe, whose definitions of real work did not include this – 'benchwork' – the activity was meaningless. He used time like this to fend off boredom. He had no inclination to instruct boys in these skills and boys had no inclination to learn.

JOE'S DISCIPLINE

Unlike the paintshop, this was not a regime based on fear. Discipline was much less rigid, boys had much more leeway to resist. The joinery shop was a long room. It was always possible to hear people approaching. Joe and Neil both wore 'noisy' shoes. Sometimes, though, if trainees had been sitting too quietly for too long, Neil would tiptoe the length of the workshop and catch them. This was different though than anything that could happen in the paintshop. It was an occasion for laughter. The joke was shared by everyone.

> *Chavvy:* Aye, yer a sly bastard when ye' get goin' Neil.
>
> *Marc* (laughing to me):
> Ken whit that bastard did the other day? We were a' skivin'. Neil takes his shoes off an' creeps up oan us. Whit a laugh.

Among supervisors, Joe had a reputation for letting boys off with murder. When I worked in knitwear, some girls noticed that ten minutes after the hooter sounded to end break, joiners were still playing football in the yard. Because an extended break was a privilege denied them, they complained to Cath. Cath rushed downstairs to find Joe. She met Tam on the stairs, intent on the same mission.

> *Tam* (to Cath):
> Ye canny allow that sort o' thing. Joe should ken better.

Within the limits and constraints of an inflexible workshop, Joe was lenient. But 'policed' by trainees and supervisors alike, the possibilities were minimal, And even when Joe did find himself with more to be angry about than Tam, his response was very different.

Joiners were working 'out' in a local school. They were partitioning a classroom and making it into two. At this point, the frame had been raised and plasterboard was being nailed to it. Joe demonstrated the technique, warning boys to hit only the nail once, and not the plasterboard which was easily dented. Marc, it seemed, had not heard. He held the nail in place, struck it, missed, then struck the plasterboard hard about twenty times. The plasterboard was hopelessly dented. Joe noticed what had happened and rushed over and took the hammer quite roughly out of Marc's hand. Firmly (but in a restrained way) he repeated that that was not how to do it. This was as angry as I ever saw Joe. He was obviously worried about it.

> *Joe* (to me later):
> God, ah didnae mean tae lose ma temper like that. Sometimes ah

forget they're jist laddies.

Joiners, then, faced a regime that was a lot less rigid than the paintshop. Joe rarely lost his temper. He rarely used wit to put boys down and demoralise them and boys did not live in constant fear of him. The atmosphere was freer, the limits of acceptable behaviour much less narrowly defined. Boys rarely bothered to stop carrying-on when Joe walked into a room and they rarely took the precautions to avoid detection that boys did in the paintshop. Disruption was public and open, not separated off and hidden from supervisors. Life here was much less uncertain and predictable.

What this meant for boys was an atmosphere which was neither challenging nor interesting. There was little to do and little to hold their attention. Disruption did not have to be hidden and it meant that boys rarely had the motivation to do it at all. And this, far from winning their commitment and acceptance, meant they were disinterested and bored. Boys' experience of joinery was then partly organised through Joe's (idiosyncratic) understanding of YOP and the way he coped with imposing on boys a scheme that he felt was unfair.

There were other reasons, too which explained why boys here were less accepting of the workshop. One structural difference between boys' workshops (and I mentioned it at the very beginning of this section) was that, unlike painters (who joined their workshop in a staggered way throughout the year), the intake of joiners happened all at once. They began together on the same day. It happened for reasons of history and of habit. Where individual painters entered an already-established work routine and had to fit themselves into an atmosphere where boys were already well-behaved and hard-working, each successive generation of joiners together and in opposition to supervisors created something that was new. Joiners learned about the workshop as a group. They were more cohesive and less prone to tactics of divide and rule. This feature of life in the joinery shop undoubtedly had a part to play in explaining why joiners were more disruptive. The relationship, though, was not a simple one. Painters starting into their workshop faced a recruitment situation similar to work: joiners experienced something a lot less novel – it felt more like school than work and was subsequently less what they wanted.

OVERALLS, 'PIECES', BREAKS

What joiners wore at work was another small detail which contributed to their feeling less than painters and slightly less satisfied with their lot. For reasons of habit and history, boys in the joinery shop were not supplied with overalls. They wore work clothes but they did not have the symbolic significance that overalls did in the paintshop. Unlike Tam, Joe never capitalised on or attributed fetishised significance to what boys wore. There were no clothes specific to joinery that were exchanged for boys' good behaviour. As much as painters, joiners wanted to be defined as real workers and as real joiners and it was for small reasons like this that it is possible to understand joiners' lesser commitment to their workshop.

In the paintshop painters were created as workers in relation to breaks and lunch and where and how they had them. This was also true for joiners. In their own space, they like nothing better than to discuss and swop 'pieces'. And in so far as joiners were integrated, they were integrated by things like this. But once again the opportunity to maximise this in the context of the joinery workshop was denied them. Arrangements for lunch were, in the eyes of the joiners, a second-best. The equivalent of the painters' 'hut' did not exist. They ate lunch in their own workshop and this denied them the full-scale fantasy about being real workers.

JOBS OUT

Supervisors and boys in the joinery loved to be on jobs. Here too, this provided them with their reasons to be. It gave boys work that was meaningful and a sense of self that they wanted. As much as for painters, they loved to jump into the van with wood and tools, hammers, saws and drills. They raised frames, laid floors, put up extensions and revelled in the whole experience. And in so far as they behaved at all, it was in order to be able to do this. They lived for the special perks times like these afforded. They particularly liked time spent in the van travelling to and from work. They finished early and took longer breaks. Most of all, it allowed them to feel like real men with real jobs. Yet there were several features about 'jobs out' in the joinery shop which meant that the experience was less satisfying for them than it was for the paintshop boys. For example, Joe was not intent on using every mechanism at his disposal to create the illusion of real work where it did not in fact exist. He never referred to these jobs as if they were commercially competitive. There was never talk about invoices and tenders. 'Jobs out' were a training exercise and boys knew it. Consequently there was much less around which boys could hang and build up personal fantasies. Joe had no intention of attempting to integrate boys on the basis of something which did not exist. In the absence of real work, the illusion of it was not created here. Hence, though boys in joinery did enjoy being out on jobs, it did not feed their wildest dreams, nor did it provide them (completely) with the cultural identity they wanted. A further aspect of 'jobs out' was that when joiners went out on a job, they all went. In the context of the joinery shop (unlike the paintshop), 'jobs out' were not something to aspire to and compete for. There was not the feeling of elation for some, disappointment for those left behind. If there was work out to be done, everybody did it. And in this sense, too, 'jobs out' felt a lot less like the pinnacle of achievement and more like a training exercise.

However the biggest problem of winning the acceptance of joiners concerned something different. For joiners, 'jobs out' were scarce. It was, I think, simply more difficult to generate the kind of jobs joiners could do 'out' than it was for painters. It is more straightforward to allow a group of boys to decorate a hall than it is to allow them to lay a floor. In all the time I was there, joiners only did two jobs out. Thus, the main thing that defined them in the joinery shop hardly ever happened. And this more than any other factor explained their lack of commitment.

JOBS IN

The role that 'jobs in' played for joiners was not unrelated to this. 'Jobs in' constituted a much larger part of their time than it did for painters. Painters found 'jobs in' meaningless (but acceptable on the basis of being a necessary evil to be tolerated at slack times). Joiners thought the same way, and much of their time was spent hanging around waiting for something which happened very infrequently. The experience of being a joiner here was subsequently both negative and boring.

This negativity surrounding 'jobs in' was further compounded because the content of 'jobs in' for joiners was even more meaningless than it was for painters. What passed for 'jobs in' in the joinery shop was 'benchwork'. A far cry from male manual labour, it smacked of school 'woodwork' and was held in contempt by supervisors and boys. Everyone experienced 'benchwork' as 'cissy', tedious and irrelevant. Aspirations were to be joiners on building sites, raising frames and staircases, building partitions and laying floorboards. Doing 'fancy joints' at a bench was what happened in schools and boys hated it.

Unlike painters, where the daily culture seemed (at least superficially) energetic and exciting, joiners' workplace culture was for the most part boring. Partly to do with Joe's personality, it was also the result of structural constraints on the nature of what it was possible for joiners to do. For even 'jobs in' allowed painters to feel busy and look productive. They had a high profile in the workshop, rushing around continually with ladders and paintbrushes. For painters, it was always possible to find something to paint (regardless of how often it had been painted before). There were simply fewer jobs for joiners to do. Joiners spent all their time in their workshop doing work that was even less meaningful than repainting the canteen. There was no commitment to benchwork in the joinery shop from supervisor or boys. The energy that went into it was small.

For example, boys were engaged on the task of making small tables throughout the time I was in Seafield. None was ever completed and no-one ever took one home. When Joe did try to pass on skills to boys in the context of the workshop, it generally fell flat. On discovering after several months that many of the boys still found it impossible to use a ruler and measure anything accurately, he tried to do something about it. Providing paper, rulers and pencils, he set a test. Boys spent hours joking about it. No-one finished it. Joe never marked it.

During my time there one ongoing task was taking old planks of wood and sawing them by hand till they were straight. The job was a 'filler' and it could have kept boys busy for years. It was picked up and left off continually, depending on what else was happening. These 'filler' jobs were used in a slightly different way here than they had been in the paintshop. Boys were still expected to look busy for visitors – and generally did. Other than that, Joe would allow them to sit around for hours, insisting they take up work only when their behaviour was disruptive enough to impinge on the rest of the workshop. Sometimes as he walked past a group of boys looking bored, he would suggest they find something to do.

Joe: Come oan you laddies, ye've done nothin' a' day.

Sometimes they would pick up work, mostly they would not. Here, 'filler' jobs appeared for what they were – boys looked busy for management, there was no game involved with supervisors.

DISRUPTION

In part, it was boys' boredom that structured their disruption. The formal content of their work was irrelevant and neither did they learn the informal things about work that so endeared the painters to their workshop. This in addition to Joe's limits being a lot less narrowly defined, meant that boys here had neither the need nor the inclination to develop the subtle, hidden culture that made life for painters interesting.

In sharp contrast to painters, the day-to-day culture of joiners was boring. The extreme aspects of their disruption that I had witnessed as an outsider happened in fact only infrequently. I spent most of my time standing in front of a heater, freezing, living in my head. Mornings I spent reading the *Daily Record* from cover to cover. Boys spent time in the same way. Hours would pass and no-one had the energy to speak. Boys would be engaged in some kind of small repetitive behaviour. Someone would be swinging on a chair for hours, some else would be rhythmically and systematically banging one nail after another into a bench, another boy would be removing the nails that had been hammered in the day before.

Chavvy sat one day and meticulously took apart a plane. He removed the blade and skillfully and neatly reduced the padded, cushioned chair to the woodwork. (Stripping a chair took on a whole new meaning!) When Joe walked by, Chavvy did not bother to stop.

Joe: That's no' very clever, is it son.

This was the hidden side of life with the joiners – the stultifying atmosphere which made up the experience of most of their working day. These long silent times were interspersed infrequently by bursts of energy. And it was this that gave the joiners their public reputation.

For example, Douggie, swinging on a chair, would suddenly fall off. This would set off a flurry of activity – as it would have in the paintshop. Douggie would pick himself up, pick up the chair, throw it around and the mêlée would spill over in to the yard. Before long they would be, for example, wheeling each other around in wheelbarrows, leaping wildly in and out of puddles. And it was at this point that Joe would react. Aware that their behaviour was visible, and more as a token gesture than anything else, Joe would suspend someone.

    Wee Rab (a painter. Humorously):

    Four o' the joiners got sent hame yesterday – they were in the canteen makin' a cup o' tea. They left the electric fire oan a' night but.

A recurring theme was swotting flies.

    Marc: There's a fly

This activity took place in the middle of winter and the flies were imaginary. The objects that were used to swot them were six-foot planks of wood. This happened infrequently and quickly died down into the usual silence and boredom. The overwhelming experience of being a joiner was of being silent and bored. The formal and informal aspects of their work were irrelevant: they lacked the necessary motivation, commitment and energy to generate a culture in opposition strong enough to overcome this general feeling.

For many reasons, then, the joiners were a lot less integrated than painters. For one thing, they were disruptive because they could be. Joe's limits were a lot more flexible than Tam's. Disruption happened also because the content of their day was less interesting. They were afforded much less of an opportunity to take on and build around the workshop an identity they strongly identified with.

The question arising from this is why in the face of all this joiners were not a lot more disruptive. Their resistance fell between several stools. They were more disruptive than painters, though their disruptive behaviour never reached the proportions of McVee (or for that matter girls, though that story is for later).

REAL MEN / REAL JOBS

Joiners wanted the same things as painters – to feel like real men with real jobs. In the context of the joinery shop this was not achievable. They were, subsequently, less satisfied. They did have, though, enough to ensure that they wanted to be in the workshop and they wanted to stay. In its own way, joiners' resistance was limited too and this can be partly explained in the fact that joiners wanted to be allowed to stay in Seafield as much as painters did. The main difference was simply the different limits set by Tam and Joe. Jointers were more disruptive because Joe allowed them to be. The bottom line for boys in both workshops was an abhorrence of a return to the dole. And the boredom and dissatisfying nature of what passed for work in the joinery shop reflected the fact that boys were in fact prepared to put up with quite a lot in order to be allowed to stay.

It would certainly be unfair to give the impression that boys got nothing out of the joinery shop. They did. It did give them some flavour of real work which allowed them partly to feel like real men. They did enjoy jobs out. The problem was that this feeling was neither strong enough nor sustained enough to integrate them completely. It was, though, enough to make them want to be there and be allowed to stay. They did, within the limits set by

Joe, behave.

I talked about painters' integration and outlined that one big factor which won their acceptance was the ability of Tam to provide jobs for boys to go on to at the end of the year. The way this worked out for joiners was slightly different. The promise and the hope of something at the end was also a big factor ensuring boys' acceptance of the joinery shop. And Joe and Neil were as successful at generating jobs for boys as Tam was – indeed, they found more jobs. However, it was not the simple generating of jobs that was the important factor for life in the paintshop. It was what Tam did with the jobs he did generate that was important. And unlike Tam, Joe never structured life for the joiners around competition for jobs. Even though there were more jobs available for joiners, boys here were less individually competitive for them. Joe never used jobs in exchange for good behaviour. Neither was there the same emphasis on references and qualifications. Boys discussed them from time to time, but there was less awareness that a good reference was closely connected to a job. Joiners as a group were much less differentiated in terms of ability. Jobs that were available were allocated more or less at random and given on the basis of things that had a lot more to do with chance and circumstances than they were to do with ability and achievement.

TO CONCLUDE

Tam wholeheartedly embraced the aims of and assumptions of YOP. He accepted that to make boys employable meant creating a regime that resembled a real workshop as closely as possible. By contrast, Joe was much less accepting of the official aims of YOP, and much more aware of its potentially exploitative aspects. Consequently, he did not push boys hard nor was he generally punitive. He created a workshop that felt a lot less like real work that the paintshop did.

The implications of this were somewhat counterintuitive. Where it is easy to be critical of the paintshop and the way boys learned skills, they *did* learn things about work that were impressive. They were rarely bored, they gained confidence in themselves and they developed a sense of themselves as manual workers. The joinery shop was not challenging in anything like the same way. Boys here were more dissatisfied and bored than painters, and they learned fewer skills and competances. It seemed, that, at least for boys, the nearer a workshop came to resembling boys' ideas of a real workshop, the more accepting of it they were, the more positive sense of themselves they received and the better they liked it.

4

BOYS AND SEXUALITY

See that burd wi' the skin heid an' the nae teeth, she's absolutely unbelievable.

Haw Hammy, did ye git it last night?

Haw Chavvy, ye still gaun' oot wi' that burd wi' the great tits?

Ah canny stand lassies wi' nae tits.

I have talked about various aspects of boys' preoccupations and culture. They came to the workshop with identities already formed. What they wanted most to be was real workers with real jobs. In the absence of this as an immediate possibility on leaving school, boys grasped the workshop as a good alternative to the dole. Apart from this, boys had one other major preoccupation – girls!

DAILY PREOCCUPATIONS AND FANTASIES

Men are defined in the world as workers. Paul Willis (1977) argued that the idea of real work is inextricably linked to ideas about masculinity. For the group I studied, work was denied them – and if you cannot be a real worker, you cannot be a real man. I want to argue that when boys cannot be workers, the implication is not a lessening of their assertion of masculinity, rather, an exaggeration. Aspects of masculine culture were heightened. The paintshop (and the joinery shop) were modelled on the idea of real workshops. In fact, they bore less of an approximation to a real workplace than a caricature of one. Boys played at being real men with real jobs. Ten boys would sit around in spartan workplace conditions and simultaneously light up ten fags. They played endless games of poker and discussed daily and ritually what they had to eat for their 'piece'. Traditional symbols, like clocking in and out, the provision of free overalls, the collection of 'wages', assumed huge, fetishised importance. In the workshop boys created themselves and were created as hard real men with hard real jobs.

The franticness and desperation they created around this was also manifest in other aspects of their lives. Aspects of their personal relationships were exaggerated and caricatured too. For example, male workplaces are renowned as places where women are objectified, discussed and ridiculed. It happened at least to the same extent in Seafield. Everyday chat inevitably returned to discussing women as objects of sex to be used and abused. Girls existed in terms of their appearance. They were pieces of anatomy, to be discussed and commented on.

Boys' feeling of inadequacy, the sense of failure they felt about their lives, was also put on to a preoccupation with sex, 'scoring' and undermining girls. In a world where there were so many material hardships for these boys (bad housing, no jobs and no money), the way they lived and laughed through their difficulties was, in so many ways, admirable. Yet it is difficult to hold on to and appreciate these positive things when so many of the ways in which they coped with their own situations was marred by sexism. So much of the energy and effort put into avoiding and diverting authority was at the same time concerned with degrading and abusing girls.

Here is one example of the way in which disruption was invariably reduced to petty sexism. A severe attack of boredom in the joinery shop was offset one day by a game of Bingo. Number boards were made from blocks of wood, numbers by hammering in nails. Chavvy was the bingo caller. He did a slick and clever job of transforming traditional Bingo calls into calls which were more relevant. Each and every call was sexist.

All the twos: tits and two, twenty-two.
One and one: skinny Liz's legs eleven.
All the sexes: sexty sex.

Their game was enterprising. But sexism was deeply ingrained in every aspect of their culture. Russell was in awful form one day. It was easy to tell. He spent the morning staring at the bench, swinging back and forth in his chair, hands in pockets. He rose only to give the locker door a periodic smash. Chavvy homed immediately into the root of the problem.

Chavvy: Ye didnae score last night did ye?
Russell: Na, she wiz feart hur auntie wid come in.

The night before had been Russell's big night. It was widely known. Failure meant that he had to cope, not only with his own disappointment, but also with the humiliation and embarrassment of facing his pals. He did, though, manage to engender a fair amount of support, sympathy and advice from his friends, who obviously identified strongly with his predicament. Practical help took the form of finding him a replacement (his girlfriend had been dropped like hot bricks for her cowardliness). Chavvy (to the rescue) confided that his own 'burd' had a 'nice lookin' pal'.

Russell: Whit's she like?
Chavvy: She's dead nice lookin' – ah'm tellin' ye!
Russell: Ah, bit – wid you go oot wi' hur?
Chavvy: Aye, ah'm tellin' ye!
Douggie: Dinnae listen tae him, ah ken hur, she's gobbin'.
Chavvy: Naw, she's really nice lookin', ah'm no' kidden'.
Russell: Well, tell me exactly whit she's like.

Chavvy: Well she's wee, goat a nice bum.

Russell: Is she thin?

Chavvy: Aye, she's thin.

Russell: Whit aboot hur hair?

Chavvy: It's broon an' wedged.

Russell: Huz she goat big tits?

Chavvy: Well, she's goat tits. Ah'm tellin' ye ah'd go oot wi' hur masel'.

John: Ah've been gaun up tae S... a lot the now, ma burd stays there – s'crawlin' wi' nice lookin' burds. Ye kin come up there wi' me if ye want.

In all the time I was with the boys, I do not think I ever heard a girl discussed in terms of anything other than her appearance or as an object of sex. Girls as people were never mentioned.

Marc: Whit's your burd like?

Douggie: Mine? Well, she's wee, goat bit tits – well quite big, goat a nice arse – ah widnae go oot wi' a burd that didnae huv a nice arse. Wears makeup, tight jeans. She's a' right.

Chavvy did not appear for work. Next day I asked him where he had been. He told me he had been up at court for 'nickin' cars'.

Me: Whit oan earth did ye start nickin' cars fur?

Chavvy (laughing, tongue in cheek):

Ah dunno'. Ah wiz depressed.

Douggie: Ye wir depressed! Yer still gaun oot wi' that wee burd wi' the big tits.

Chavvy: Aye.

Douggie: An' yer depressed! How kin ye be depressed when yer gaun oot wi' a burd wi' tits like that?

Chavvy: Aye ah ken. We're supposed tae be gettin' engaged in March.

Douggie (can hardly speak for laughing):

Yer whit! Yer gettin; engaged! Away an' no' be stupit.

Marc (smugly):

Ah ken why he's getting' engaged. There's only one reason anybody gets engaged. Ye get it easier if yer engaged.

Chavvy leant back smugly in his chair and did not deny it. John entered into the conversation at this stage. He used to be in the joinery workshop. After his year he went to do WEEP with a local decorating firm.

John: Aye, ah could imagin' masel' gettin' engaged – but ah'd never, ever git married. Some o' tha' boys at ma work, ye want tae hear them, they'd put ye off fur life. Some o' them are only twenty, an' some o' them have been married fur years – an' they fuckin' hate, they fuckin' *hate* their wives. Ye want tae hear some o' the things they say aboot them. They dinnae even get oot fur a pint. Their wives jist go oan at them the whole time. They fuckin' *hate* their wives.

SEXISM

Much of what is absorbed, the whole of their culture, inside and out of Seafield, is laced with sexism. Craigie arrived one day with a tape recorder borrowed from his father. It was played in the workshop for one entire day. First one side, then the other, then back to the beginning. It was a live recording of a night club spot by a local comedian. Listening to the tape was, for the boys, a relatively unimportant event. These feelings were reinforced and validated by supervisors (who also enjoyed the tape). The tape was particularly appreciated because the comedian was local, so he had accents and mannerisms like their own. He began with a series of racist jokes (against blacks, Jews and Irish people). This was followed by a series of anti-gay jokes, then a whole lot more about and against women. The only jokes about 'normal people' (white, heterosexual men) celebrated drunkenness, which were the jokes on which the tape ended.

I spent the whole of that day with my stomach in knots of anger and frustration. Futile attempts to protest were interpreted as prudish and served only to double my anguish. The boys strutted around smugly, feeling like real men, revelling in 'normality'. From every side these boys absorbed abusive and objectified images and messages about women. They picked it up from the daily banter which existed amongst themselves, from fathers and brothers at home, as well as from external sources of popular culture – television, cinema, and to an increasing extent from the soft porn videos they spent so much time watching with their friends and families. The culture is extended into the workshop where boys endlessly discuss what they have been watching, what is available and worth seeing.

> *Pete:* Huv' ye seen this yin called ... Well there's a bit in it where ye actually see them cuttin' this wumin up. Ye should get it, ah'm no' kiddin', it's absolutely horrible.

It is important not to lose sight of the implications of all of this for girls. The preoccupation and obsessions of men/boys, their needs and fantasies, were concerned with women as objects. As the material conditions of men's/boys' lives worsen, these tend to escalate and be exaggerated.

A short discussion about my own experience of Seafield might be valid here. I was in the presence of teenagers constantly for five months. When I began I was unaffected by thoughts of my appearance. By the time I left, I was paranoid. The ideal standard (to which all of the girls aspired and several came close to achieving) was to be blonde, with flicked back hair, to wear make-up, tight stretch jeans, flimsy sandals and thin jackets, and to weigh a pre-pubescent seven-and-a-half stones. I was not alone in weighing considerably more, wearing baggy jeans and sweat shirts, ankle boots and heavy jackets, and those of us like this suffered together. It is one thing to accept that teenage girls are nothing but the way they look, but to experience it (or, as in my case, to re-experience it) hammered home the slogan very firmly.

> *Kenny:* Colour's ye'r hair Trish?

Trish: S'fire red. S'barry, eh?

Kenny: Aye. Whit colour wiz it before?

Trish: Ah'd it blonde. Ah like it a' different colours.

Kenny: Dae you dye ye'r hair, Anne?

Me: Nut.

Trish: Dae ye' like it the way it is?

Me: Oct, no' really, ah never really think aboot it.

Trish: Dae ye' always wear it up?

Me: Naw, jist in here.

Trish: It'd be better doon. Ah always take mine doon at lunchtime, you should tae Anne.

Comments like these hurt. I felt worthless. Girls generally were not unaware of the unfairness and oppressiveness of the structures of their worlds

Trish: Ye should wear make-up Anne. Lassies dae look better wi' make-up oan.

Pete: Lassies look absolutely gobbin' wi'oot make-up. If ma burd came doon the stairs tae go oot wi' me wi'oot any oan, ah'd send hur right back up tae pit it oan. Ah widnae go oot wi' hur.

Trish: Ah widnae go oot the door wi'oot ma make-up oan. Ma ma disnae even see me wi'oot ma make-up. Even if ah huv' a bath, the first thing ah dae is tae go an' pit it right back oan. Wi'oot it ma face is dead white, an' ah've gaot dead wee horrible eyes.

Me: Oct ye dae nut Trish. Ye widnae look any different wi'oot make-up. Ah think lassies wear make-up cause laddies expect ye tae. It's jist whit folk think 'nice-lookin' is, it disnae make any difference really.

Trish: Aye ah ken. If naebody hud ever wore make-up ever, then it wid be OK no' tae wear it. But everybody does wear it an' ah'm no' gaun' tae be the only burd no' wearin' it. Ah'd feel really shitty.

See ma pal Pammy. Like, if ah'm gaun oot wi' hur, she'll never come up for me. Ah've tae ai'ways go doon tae hur bit so she kin see whit ah've goat oan – then she kin wear somethin' better. Jackie wid never dae that tae me, but some lassies ur like that. See you, Anne, yer dead naïve.

I knew the personal cost to me of being a 'girl' in the workshop. Yet I was twice as old, numerous times materially better off, surer of myself and my life than anyone else. I still found this aspect of the workshop an extremely undermining experience.

Me: My God, you lot are disgusting. Ye's are sittin' aboot here talkin' aboot lassies as if they were like a bunch o' animals or something'.

Chavvy (unabashed, laughing):

Aye, ah ken, we're awffy, we're talkin' aboot them like they wiz big slabs o' meat.

The effect of this on sixteen-year-old girls I will discuss in a later chapter.

5

KNITWEAR

'Knitwear' generally held twenty or so girls and three supervisors. There were three separate but connected areas, each with a supervisor in charge of half a dozen or so girls. If boys learned skills that were traditionally male, girls were offered a skill that was as distinctly and traditionally feminine. They learned to operate small knitting machines. Each area possessed a machine for every girl, sewing machines, ironing board and iron – every inch a workplace and an environment for girls.

PROCESS OF ACCEPTANCE

When I first arrived in Seafield I spent my first few days in the office. I felt awkward and disoriented, observing trainees from this safe distance and trying (unsuccessfully) to imagine a role for myself. From the office I moved to knitwear, spending two weeks there before it was decided that I should accompany Trish to the paintshop. My main time in knitwear was at the end of my time in the workshop, after I had been with painters and joiners.

I was initially in knitwear when I felt new and awkward in the workshop generally, and I felt as uncomfortable among the girls as I later did with boys (though not for the same reasons). I felt out of place and ignored and I had little faith that I would ever get to know any of them. From my fieldnotes: 'I honestly don't know how I'm doing. Sometimes I feel that they will accept me, sometimes I feel like a nuisance, sometimes I think they quite like me being around, sometimes I feel in the way.' This largely understates the depths of my insecurity. This was the beginning of my fieldwork. A lot hinged on it. Another snippet from my fieldnotes captures more honestly how I felt: 'They don't like me, they'll never like me, I don't fit in. They think I'm horrible.' It felt to me that my presence prevented them from doing what they wanted to do, from saying what they wanted to say. I was wrong, and only with hindsight did I come to understand their initial response. During my first week there all I did know was that no-one was speaking to me. When they did, it was merely to elicit the information they needed to place me.

Because I was small and wore no make-up they assumed I was young. The fact that I did not wear 'trendy' clothes (rather, jeans and a duffel coat) meant I was not interested in boys. They assumed I was naïve and immature. They saw me and related to me from the very first as someone who was not too different from themselves, the same age, from the same background, a bit slow and wet behind the ears. They ignored me initially, as they ignored *all* new trainees.

Towards the end of my first two weeks, there were an increasing number of small signs that suggested I was being accepted. A slap on the back from Linda on the way past, a joke made at my expense.

Lena: God, Anne, yer slow oan the uptake.

Fran: Bet Anne wid never dae a thing like that, eh!

I ended my first stint in knitwear with an increasing understanding of the way the workshop was organised, of the role I was creating for myself and that was being created for me. In many ways it was untimely that I was whisked away for two-and-a-half months to be with Trish and the boys.

My time with painters and joiners had left me feeling unconfident and undermined. Between workshops I took a week's holiday. Throughout the week I was anxious about my return to knitwear. The night before I did not sleep. I thought carefully about what I could wear. Having wandered around with painters in overalls and jumpers, I was nervous about joining the girls who all looked glamorous. I knew whatever I wore would be subject to comment and I would feel awful. In the paintshop I had been defined as Trish's kind, dull-witted pal. I was aware that in knitwear my role would be similar, and to be defined in any situation as someone who is dowdy is undermining. On the plus side, I started back in knitwear without fear of rejection. By then I was a familiar and accepted part of Seafield. I knew all the girls and had talked regularly with them. Some of them I knew well, all of them had an idea of what I was like. I also knew I would be integrated into the group in a way that participant observers seldom are – as part of the outgroup.

Classically, participant observers make for the ringleaders. In my case this was impossible. I neither looked, nor could I play, the right part. There were, however, a number of girls in the same boat. They neither looked punky, nor did they look glamorous. Like me, they wore jeans and jumpers. They felt bad about their appearance in relation to other girls and felt bad about themselves in relation to boys. They were very decidedly the outgroup and I was very firmly part of it.

An incident happened during my first week back in the workshop which affirmed, to me at any rate, who my friends were going to be. Mary was quiet and wore brown cords and a brown jumper continually. She was far from being popular. If anything was stolen everyone immediately thought of Mary. She knitted very little and showed little interest in learning. She kept herself to herself and had few friends. One day, when I had been in the workshop only a short time, she pulled me aside.

Mary: Ah'm scunnered wi' this place. After break, ah'm no' comin' back.

I chatted to her for a bit, assuming that what she had told me was common knowledge. When the hooter went at break she made a special point of saying 'cheerio' to me. I was totally unprepared for the fuss her absence caused in the afternoon.

Cath (supervisor):
Where's Mary? Has anyone seen Mary?

It was only when Cath phoned her mother that anyone realised that Mary was not coming back. I was the only person in the workshop who had known about it.

Louise, Jen, Ruby and Pat became my special friends. They were quiet and unconfident – the girls who did not make it in anyone's terms, least of all their own. And somewhat uncharacteristically (for participant observers) I was closest to, and came to understand best, girls whose culture, lives and expectations remained (usually) most hidden. And it was from this vantage point that I came to understand the culture of the ringleaders and the workshop in general. I did not regret it. Unorthodox it may have been in terms of classic participant observation studies, but I relaxed about it when it quickly became apparent that the 'outgroup' had no less a finger on the pulse of the workings of Seafield than the 'ingroup' had. The ringleaders were visible enough and I had every opportunity to observe their behaviour. Without my close association with the outgroup, however, the finer points of *their* lives would surely, and as usual, have been missed.

I had high expectations of what I wanted from the workshop the second time around; I was surer of what I wanted to create and more confident that I would not reproduce earlier mistakes. Initially I had been nervous about attaching myself to one room. I was anxious about being identified with any particular group in case that would limit my access to general information. At that time I did not have a machine of my own, rather I spent my time wandering between workshops, helping out in small ways – sweeping up, pressing garments, sewing ribs.

I had an inkling at that time that conversations between girls were mainly about boys and boyfriends (teenage girls are supposed to be preoccupied by that sort of thing and also I had at one time spent a great deal of time doing it myself). Initially I saw no evidence of it. Little conversation was directed at me personally. What I overheard was mainly about clothes and records.

Fairly quickly I realised that my strategy was not ideal. Defining myself as someone with this kind of freedom (to move between workshops, not being tied to a machine) set me apart from girls and opened the door to future resentment. It was an obstacle to getting to know any of them really well. I simply did not stay in one workshop long enough to build up close relationships. In effect, I took the easy way out. When girls wanted to have private conversations they merely had to wait until I disappeared. And rather than push relationships, I made it easy for girls to exclude me. Friendships remained on a fairly superficial level. So I attached myself to one room and, by doing so, to one particular group of girls. I was allocated a knitting machine and learned to use it in much the same way as any other trainee.

In knitwear girls were not allocated to rooms randomly. Cath was the head supervisor and had a reputation for being strict. She kept the most unruly girls with her to keep an eye on them. Girls nearing the end of their time in the workshop were in Sue's room. They knitted mostly Fair Isle. In Margaret's room were girls who were quieter, girls who were unsuccessful in their own eyes and in the eyes of their peers. And it was no accident that I was allocated to this room and that it was with these girls that I became firm friends.

In Margaret's room I learned to thread the machine and I struggled with my first scarf. When the going got tough Louise, the trainee who sat at the next machine, came to help. She would push me aside, shake her head at my stupidity and pick up my dropped stitches. She pulled back the rows I had knitted in the wrong colour and picked up my work from the floor when I had swept every stitch off the machine. This probably represented the only power Louise had in the world. She liked her role in relation to me and we became close. Jen started in the workshop a week later than me. Her machine was on my other side. And while she cursed and swore and swept her knitting on to the floor, I would patiently hang her stitches on to the machine. Louise, Jen and I were all friends. Ruby detested knitting. She was rough, tough and had had a hard life. She never managed to knit anything passable. She had an amazing sense of humour and kept us amused for hours. All four of us spent a lot of time together.

From this basis, the conversations about boys which I initially only guessed were happening around me, gradually crept up on me. At first I merely heard snatches as I passed by girls talking on the balcony or in the toilet. Suddenly, almost overnight, I had enough information about girls to know what they were talking about and to participate. From then on I never talked about anything else. We pooled together bits and pieces of information about boys, discussed who was 'fanciable' and who was not and what to do about it. And once again I participated as someone who was young, naïve, neither knowledgeable about nor into boys.

GIRLS' SUPERVISORS

Before talking about girls, I want to talk about their supervisors.

> *Cath*: The most we can do for them in Seafield is to be able to write a reference at the end that says – she attended, she was punctual, she worked hard – and it is, actually, a lot.

I have already discussed how attitudes like these worked themselves out in relation to supervisors and boys in the paintshop. This attitude had different implications in the context of girls. Boys' supervisors were working-class and tradesmen, hired on the basis of trade skills. They passed on these skills to boys in a way boys strongly identified with. Girls' supervisors, too, were hired on the basis of practical skills. Cath had spent most of her adult life as a single parent, struggling to support herself by knitting on a small knitting machine at home. Like Tam, she had trade contacts of her own and supplied local craft shops with jumpers. Like Tam, many of these contacts were friends. These skills and contacts she brought with her to Seafield. The stripey and Fair Isle patterns she had originally used (and that were so popular with the middle classes and tourists in town) were the basis of what was now knitted in the workshop. Her old contacts (craft fairs, stalls, local shops) were outlets for what was knitted. Margaret, too, had spent most of her married life at home. Part of her working life had been spent as a demonstrator and sales representative for a firm who sold knitting machines. Sue had a college background and was also a skilled knitter who had a machine at home. The similarity with boys' workshops was more apparent than real, though, and the way in which supervisors and girls related was fundamentally different.

Cath

Though all three supervisors had different ideas about girls and how the workshop should be organised, Cath was the senior supervisor and discipline in the workshop was generally mediated through her.

Although most of my time was spent in Margaret's room, Cath was the supervisor I felt personally closest to and most identified with. Like Joe, Cath was fairly sceptical of YOP, and like him, she lived a lot of contradictions. She coped with them in a different way from Joe. Cath's roots were working-class. She understood and empathised with girls and genuinely cared about trainees. She was often the first to draw my attention to things about the circumstances of trainees' lives that would interest me. Caring, though, in the context of such schemes took on (and had to take on) specific forms. This is best illustrated by example.

Cath first drew my attention to Tina and pointed out to me that Tina was not altogether what she seemed. On the surface Tina seemed like the trainee with the least problems. She was always immaculately dressed and had boundless energy. In the workshop she was loud, noisy and funny. People either loved Tina or hated her. She was fairly productive in terms of knitting, but most of her time was taken up talking, annoying people or thinking about ways to annoy people. She seemed not to have a care in the world. Nothing could have been further from the truth. And over time I gathered enough information to determine that her life had not been easy. Tina had six siblings and she was the oldest. Her father was a drunk and had made life at home intolerable. He was violent and had deprived the family of money. Eventually Tina's mother had thrown him out. His influence over their lives had not stopped there and over the past few years he frequently returned to the house to beat up the family and ransack the house. To support the family, Tina's mum had three jobs – she cleaned the local school from six until eight in the morning, worked in a shop during the daytime and had another cleaning job at night. Tina loved her mum and she took a lot of responsibility at home for the younger children.

Cath knew this and first drew my attention to it, and unlike other supervisors who disliked Tina, Cath was tolerant. Tina's mum was in fact, and not surprisingly, ill. Her stomach was incredibly swollen and she had a lot of lumps. She could not eat. She was nervous about going to a doctor and anxious that if she had to go to hospital, this would be catastrophic for the family. She was afraid of losing her jobs and afraid that her husband would take advantage of her absence to return home. Tina had spent a lot of time talking to Cath about it. She suggested that Tina put a lot of energy into persuading her mother to see a doctor. Tina succeeded and took a morning off work to accompany her. And although no-one doubted the validity of Tina's excuse for being late, it resulted in a long discussion among supervisors about whether or not she should have her wages docked. She did in fact lose a morning's wages. Cath justified it like this:

> *Cath*: I know Tina had a good excuse but if you start letting one of them off with excuses like this you'd have to let them all off. It would be chaos.

The incident did nothing to endear supervisors to Tina.

> *Tina*: Fuckin' bastards, they're oan yer backs the whole time. Ye' get away wi' nothin' in this place.

Behind Cath's caring attitude lay the ideology of the workshop. For their own good, for the good of their employability, it was necessary to be strict. In the context of Seafield a genuine concern for trainees and their welfare took on an element that was strongly coercive. Ideas about YOP and YTS built into Cath a strong conviction that to be kind, to make them employable, first of all you have to be cruel. In many ways Cath was the strictest of all the supervisors. And she illustrated this very directly in relation to Tina.

> *Cath*: When I first came here I used to get really upset when girls came in and told me they were late because they'd been up all night cause their mothers had been getting beaten up or something. I used to get upset for their mothers and be really soft. Now I'm really hard. I put trainees first and tell them to put themselves and their jobs first. No employer would take that as an excuse and we can't do it here. If you were late for work all the time because your father beat up your mother, you'd get your books, no question. So I make them come in here, no matter what's happening at home. They're better off here anyway.

In their own interests, in the interests of keeping them off the streets, for their own protection and future job prospects, Cath created a regime that was strict and authoritarian. Girls were never allowed home early, and they never had long breaks. Limits of behaviour were narrowly defined and trainees were suspended and docked for very little.

Joyce had been noisy and had been playing up all day. A box of pins had been dropped on the floor and Cath had told her to pick them up. Joyce ignored Cath and a shouting match ensued.

Joyce: Ah didnae drop them an' ah'm no' pickin' them up.

Cath ended the argument by asserting that unless she picked them up she'd be suspended.

Joyce: This is too much. Ye're gunnae suspend me fur no' pickin' up a box o' pins. Some fuckin' place this, s'like a fuckin' prison.

Joyce eventually picked up the pins but got herself suspended later in the day for refusing to clean out the bucket in the toilet.

Joyce: Ye're askin' me tae clean oot the bucket in the toilet. Ah no' daein' that, it's crawlin' wi' maggots. You widnae clean it oot either.

Margaret

Margaret was the newest of the supervisors. She had started the job only a month or so before I came to the workshop. My own role in relation to Margaret was somewhat difficult. Though I disagreed with her, I respected her kindness in relation to trainees and her willingness to help in relation to me. She spent a lot of time teaching me to knit, to use the machine. She corrected my mistakes, suggested patterns and colours for the things I did knit and gave me every freedom to do what I wanted in her workshop. I was extremely grateful.

At fifty, Margaret had spent a lot of her married life bringing up one child. Her husband had never wanted her to work. Only when he died did she take on a full-time job. Margaret had led a sheltered life and found girls in the workshop something of a shock.

Margaret: I had no idea girls like this existed before I came here, some of them have had terrible lives. It took me a long time to get used to it.

When her husband died, Margaret resented that she had to go out to work and she firmly believed that the place for married women was in the home.

Margaret: I blame unemployment on the women. I spent all my married life at home and that's where all women should be. Cath doesn't agree with that right enough.

The background that Margaret brought to the workshop meant that she was genuinely shocked by girls, at their behaviour and at what she knew about their lives.

The myth about youth employment – that it is the young people themselves who are the problem – is widespread, and Margaret was the representative of this view *par excellence*. Far from seeing trainees like ordinary teenagers who are jobless, girls took on the character something like pupils at a List D school. For Margaret, the reason for young people being in Seafield was because they were deficient and delinquent. Ironically, in spite of and partly because of these views, Margaret felt sympathy for trainees. Subsequently she created in her workshop a regime that was a lot less strict than Cath's. Margaret was soft and, with a few notable exceptions, the quietest and least disruptive of the trainees (including me) were in her room. Somewhat surprisingly, in their own way trainees protected her from the worst aspects of their lives.

Margaret operated a swear box, on a sliding scale according to the seriousness of the word used. And indeed, most of the money collected had been collected for minor violations. Margaret was so genuinely upset and hurt by trainees' swearing that they rarely used the worst words in her presence. Margaret often talked about them as though they were naughty children. She would have been horrified to discover how sexually experienced many of them were and at the adult responsibilities many of them had.

Ruby was one of the toughest trainees. She had been involved with a boy who had been charged with serious assault and Ruby had been (so she said) with the boy when the incident had happened. She took one day off to appear in court. She told me about it later.

> *Ruby*: God, it wiz that embarrassin'. Ye'll never believe it. Ah've never been sae embarrassed in ma whole life. Ma 'ex' wiz supposed tae huv' beaten this guy up, right. An' ah'm supposed tae go along an' say that he couldnae huv' done it cause he wiz wi' me, right. An' this guy asks me whit we wir' daein' – ah mean, ah jist look at the guy – ah wiz that embarrassed, ah couldnae believe he's asked me – CHRIST – whit did he think we wir' daein'? Playin' cairds?

Margaret seemed blissfully ignorant of the heavier aspects of Ruby's life.

> *Margaret*: Ruby's got an' awffy tongue in her head. Underneath though she's as good as gold.

Trainees related to her as some kind of soft mark aunt. They pushed her, wound her up, but they did have their limits. And they did appreciate her care. Margaret sucked sweets throughout the day and she always handed them round to girls. If someone did not have lunch (usually this meant that they had spent their money on cigarettes), Margaret would give them money and send them to the shop to buy some. If someone had a sore throat, she would send them to the shop for lozenges. Margaret related to them as though they were deprived and needy. She reacted to it by mothering them. Outside the workshop she worried about them all the time.

I will use a particular incident to illustrate how discipline worked in this workshop. Margaret's concern was mediated through Cath's strictness. The background to this story is again Ruby. This time it is a concern about her attendance and her punctuality. It was the particular week when Ruby had already had time off to appear in court. Throughout the week she had complained of toothache and had already taken a morning off because of it. Like many working-class people with a history of bad dentistry, the experience of going to a dentist is a rare event taking place only infrequently and then only usually with the onset of toothache and a tooth which has to be removed. Ruby was terrified. She was prepared to suffer the pain of toothache rather than go to a dentist. This attitude evoked no sympathy from supervisors. They penalised her heavily and would not accept toothache as an excuse for being off work. Margaret had had regular and good dental treatment all her life. At fifty-one, she had not yet lost a tooth. She was thoroughly bewildered at Ruby's attitude. Cath felt the same.

> *Cath*: I've got no sympathy. I just don't understand how someone can be in that much pain and not go to a dentist.

The saga of Ruby's tooth dragged on for days, Ruby taking more and more time off work because of it. When she was in, she was in no state to work and nothing anyone could say would induce her to go to the dentist. After a few more days of this, Ruby came in one day and announced that she had been up all night with toothache and that she would go to the dentist. Too scared to go on her own and with no one at home to take her, she had brought the problem to the workshop. Having procrastinated so much, however, the question of whether or not Ruby should be *allowed* to go was now at issue.

> *Cath*: In a real job, you have to go to the dentist in your own time. I'll let her make an appointment, but she'll have to go in her lunch break.

This decision was taken on the basis of a principle. Even through the agony of toothache, trainees (for their own good) were taught work discipline. Ruby meanwhile spent the morning sitting by the heater, a woollen glove pressed to her face. She did no work that morning. An irrational outcome of the conflict between care and coercion that operated in the workshop became even more irrational. Margaret gave up her lunch break to take Ruby to the dental hospital. They were both gone for a couple of hours. When Ruby came back she was deathly pale, dazed and in a state of shock. The event had obviously been physically and psychologically traumatic. Again a decision was made not to send her home. Familiar murmurings went up among trainees.

> *Jen*: They widnae let ye' go hame in this place even if ye' were deed.

Supervisors' justifications were different.

> *Cath*: There'd be nobody at home. She's better off here.

Margaret made up a bed for her of fur fabric and woollen blankets beside the heater. Ruby slept for hours. I was worried about her. She was tiny (she weighed six stones) and I knew she had eaten no food since six in the evening the night before. A 'normal' dose of anaesthetic in conjunction with her terror of dentists had been too much. By mid-afternoon, however, Ruby was sitting up. She still looked dazed and pale. Kindly, Margaret sent Ruby along to the canteen for hot milk. I happened to be walking along the balcony as Ruby was walking back with the milk. She staggered and lunged towards me. Just as I reached her and took the milk, she fainted. I dragged her back to the workshop and she lay down. Once again she was out cold. Jan (the staff officer) eventually came and drove her home. This time Ruby's wages were not docked. Though not dead, she was seen to have a legitimate excuse!

Sue

Sue had been hired on the basis of a qualification from textile design college in the hope of injecting creativity (in the form of new designs for jumpers and new patterns) into what girls produced. At twenty-four she was younger than I was, though (in a traditional sense) and in the eyes of the trainees, she was more accomplished. She was tall, blonde and slim. She had a house in the suburbs, a car and a husband.

The workshop had been a rude awakening for Sue as it had been for Margaret. Unlike Margaret, I think Sue had unambiguous feelings about most of the girls and had little understanding of their lives. The overriding factor for her was that they hated knitting, worked little and 'skived'. She saw them as lazy and felt that they did little to help themselves. To her, Seafield was offering girls a good opportunity and most of them were throwing it away.

Trainees felt ambiguously about her. Of all the supervisors, Sue had the most antagonistic relationship with them. There were continual references to the hard time Sue had to begin with, when she saw her main task as designing and she had not been able to handle girls and their attitudes to work. Now she followed a different strategy. She was tough. Girls both envied and hated her. The situation was most pronounced in relation to Tina. As we noted, Tina had had a hard life and she took on a lot of family responsibilities – looking after children, putting money into the house, being protective of her mother. In her own way, Tina had ambitions for herself. She wanted to get out of her situation and she did not want to end up in the same mess as her mother was in. In this she was single-minded. Like her mother, Tina worked herself into the ground. She too had three paid jobs – the 'job' in the workshop and two cleaning jobs. She gave a large chunk of her wages to her mum and the rest went on her appearance. She contrived to spend as little as possible on food, rarely eating lunch and being very nervous if she had to buy anything else. Unlike the rest of the girls, Tina had no interest in boys. She intuitively grasped that a boyfriend would hinder her plans for her life rather than help them on their way. Tina's driving ambition was money and more than anything in the world Tina wanted a full-time job.

Sue only saw one side of Tina. To her, Tina was superficial and 'on the make', interested only in money and clothes. Tina seemed loud-mouthed and aggressive; her personal ambition, her drive to 'get on' were distasteful to her.

Sue: Tina's so mercenary. She never thinks of anything but money. She makes me sick sometimes. I came in here the other day and she was actually sitting counting her money. I wouldn't be surprised if she was taking home forty pounds a week now.

Tina rose every morning at six fifteen to get herself ready to come to the workshop. In the evening she cleaned offices from five until eight. For a sixty-hour week, Tina's take-home pay would have been less than forty pounds a week.

I think the main impact Sue had on trainees was neither intended nor deliberate. When Sue chatted to trainees, she talked about her own life, about her husband, her possessions. And unlike Cath or Margaret, she was envied by the trainees. What she had was beyond their wildest dreams. Sue's very presence in the workshop, her appearance, her confident manner, stood in sharp contrast to their own lives. It did little to build up their confidence. Sue was young and newly married. She had recently moved into a new house and, bit by bit, was acquiring things for it. She often went shopping in her lunch break. On her return, trainees invariably asked her what she had in the bag. Often it was some very expensive item of furnishing or clothing from some very expensive store.

> *Sue*: We're having some people over at the weekend for dinner. I bought this dress to wear.

> *Sue*: I thought this would look good in our sitting room.

The world of home-ownership, dinner parties and even sitting rooms was beyond trainees. They were fascinated by Sue's stories about her life, but they would comment about it when she was not there.

> *Louise*: Wha' diz she 'hink she is – the queen mother or some'at?

Part of the fascination of Sue came from the fact that she *was* newly married. She talked a lot about John, her husband, about their friends, about the things they did together, their holidays skiing and so on. Still caught up in the newness of it herself, she enjoyed talking about it to trainees. One day they persuaded her to bring in her wedding photographs. The wedding had taken place in a cathedral. It was a grand, polished, tasteful affair. Sue's parents had flown over from Canada to be there. Everything was perfect. The weather was bright and sunny. Sue looked like a princess. Trainees were impressed. To them it was something that happened in Hollywood. Next day Jen brought in *her* most important photographs – her sister's twenty-first birthday party.

> *Jen*: Ma ma wanted tae gie her a big pairty. She didnae get a right weddin' 'cause she'd a'ready hud the wean.

Jen produced a more lively, if less polished, set of photographs. Kodak snaps, shaky and blurred, men with pint mugs, their arms round women. Couples danced in the background in a hall that was dingy and dark. Jen was unabashed and passed around her photographs as eagerly as had Sue. The contrast was poignant. In all, the effect of Sue's presence and behaviour on trainees was to undermine them and make them feel bad about their own lives.

> *Linda*: Huv' you ever thought aboot suicide Sue?

> *Sue*: Look, get on with your work, I don't want to hear this nonsense.

Linda: Ah huv', a' the time. Ah hate ma life. Ah wish ah wiz deed. Ah wish ye' could start again. Dae you ever wish ye' were deed Sue?
Sue: No, I'm quite content with my life really. Well I'm not quite. I will be when John and I move into our new house, it's a really fantastic house.

TO CONCLUDE

All three supervisors then were very different. Together, they seemed more involved in and concerned about the personal aspects of trainees' lives and their welfare than were boys' supervisors. What was set up here was less an impersonal employer and employee relationship than a welfare model. Supervisors related to trainees as having problems, and the role they took on was a counselling one. However, 'care' in the context of the workshop took on a flavour which was authoritarian and strict.

6

THE NATURE OF GIRLS' WORK

DISRUPTION AND CONFRONTATION

Generally in the workshop, girls' behaviour was held in low regard.

Joe: Tha' lassies are really outrageous, ah'm no' kidden' ye'. Ye' walk in there an' they're cursin' an' swearin' at supervisors. Ah've heard folk swear, but ah'm tellin' ye', ah never ken't women could swear like that till ah came here. Some o' them are really uncouth. Ah'm shocked, ah'm tellin' ye'.

Robbie: Tha' lassies are that aggressive it's no' funny.

Neil: Ken whit tha' lassies are up tae noo? They've spent the whole day leanin' owr the balcony spittin' oan boys.

Inside the workshop, the atmosphere was confrontational. In contrast to the paintshop where boys seemed mature and productive, girls were noisy. They were locked into continual battles with supervisors, regardless of who was there. Far from giving the impression of a real workplace, knitwear most resembled a sewing class at school.

Louise: Dae ye' no' think this place is jist like school? Ah dae! They're oan yer' backs the whole time.

Ally: Ah hate this place, it's jist like school. It's too strict. An' everybody, ma uncle, ma ma, everybody gits mad when ah tell them whit ye've tae dae an' whit ye've tae pit up wi' fur yer' twenty-three pounds. An' they pay yer' wages intae the bank ye' ken, it's a real hassle.

Jen: Ah'm bored stiff here. Ah used tae 'hink it wiz snobs came here – bit ah hate it.

Of all the trainees in the workshop, girls were seen to be by far the most unruly. Given that Cath operated a discipline structure that was almost as tight as Tam's, this was somewhat surprising.

Training was more formal here than in any other workshop. Everyone learned to knit on the machine, machine-sew seams, hand-sew ribs, finish and press. They knitted first simple garments and proceeded to more complicated ones. Garments were characteristically stripes or Fair Isle. Four of each type of garment had to be completed before trainees were allowed to move on to the next. They knitted first scarves, then hats, socks, jumpers, all in stripes. Then they learned to punch cards for the machine which enabled them to knit Fair Isle. Garments were sold ultimately as seconds in local shops or at local craft fairs.

Unlike for boys, it is difficult to discuss the nature of work in knitwear without discussing it in relation to the continual battle over work which raged between supervisors and girls. Boys' disruption was, for the most part, separated off and sporadic. Girls' disruption was an integral part of most of their day. At the level of the workshop itself, there were many mechanisms and techniques available to supervisors attempting to win the consent of girls. These succeeded or failed to a greater or lesser extent.

KEEPING YOUR OWN GARMENT

Trainees were allowed to buy the first of every new garment they knitted for the price of the wool (they were allowed to keep for themselves the first scarf, the first hat, the first jumper they knitted). As an added incentive, with this garment, they were allowed to put together the choice of colours and patterns they wanted. In many ways allowing trainees to keep the first of everything they knitted was no loss. No matter how hard trainees tried, first garments were rarely perfect. And indeed, trainees often did put a lot into learning how to knit a new garment when they knew it was for themselves. It meant that other garments were of better quality than they might otherwise have been. Without this incentive, trainees might never have learned to knit anything well. For example, when Ally came to knit her first Fair Isle (she had already been in the workshop for five months) she was an avid fan of the group 'Siouxie and the Banshees'. She persuaded Cath to allow her to knit a Siouxie jumper. Ally brought in one of her album covers and Cath spent a long time transferring the pattern on to graph paper and helping Ally to punch the pattern on to the card for the machine. Ally eventually knitted a very impressive jumper in black, with the profile of her favourite singer in black and white. Ally was proud of her jumper. She had put a lot into learning to knit and was a better knitter because of it. With other girls the tactic was much less successful and rather than put together the colours and patterns they wanted, they would put together patterns and colours that were easiest. Yvonne knitted her first jersey for her father (she said!). It was plain black.

MACHINES AS ISOLATION

Where the nature of boys' work often involved them being active and working on their own, this rarely happened with girls. Girls were always in one room, knitting or finishing off. Supervisors were always present. Supervisors struggled as much as possible to keep girls at their machines and girls tried to find ways to make space for themselves away from them.

Machines were noisy and isolating and girls preferred to get together and have fun. They attempted to minimise the amount of time spent on machines and to maximise the amount of time they spent 'finishing off'. They preferred pressing and sewing up to being on the machines. Sewing machines were in short supply so waiting to use them meant a chance to hang about talking to pals. Hand sewing was probably girls' favourite activity. It provided an opportunity to wander around looking for pins or scissors and the chance to sit around the heater in groups, chatting (there were seldom fewer than five or six girls at the heater at any one time). Girls aimed to get off machines as quickly as possible and to spend as much time as possible hand sewing and finishing off. Supervisors tried to keep them at their machines. Invariably girls spent more time off the machines than on them. They used many strategies to make space for themselves away from work. They deliberately fouled the machines and they bent the combs, thus jamming the machines.

DECIDING WHAT TO KNIT

There was a gap between what supervisors wanted girls to knit and what girls themselves wanted to do. Supervisors pushed girls to knit complicated garments – Fair Isle jerseys with patterns that seldom repeated and with as many colours as possible. Girls aimed to knit nothing at all.

> *Margaret:* Ruby, you've done one hat and scarf since last week. It's really outrageous. Yvonne's nearly finished four jerseys.
> *Ruby:* Ah huv' nut. Ah've did much mair than that. Ah jist forgot tae put it oan ma sheet.
> *Margaret:* That's a lie. Where are they? Show me!

Girls and supervisors continually battled over what was to be knitted, what colours were to be used and how long it was to take them.

> *Margaret:* Jen, we need jerseys.
> *Jen:* Ah fuckin' knitted a jersey yesterday – ah'm knittin' a scarf!
> *Margaret:* Jen, we need jerseys.
> *Jen:* Well, ah'm no fuckin' daein' it – ask wan o' them through there.
> *Margaret:* I'm not telling you again, start a jersey.
> *Jen:* Well if ah knit a jumper, ah'm knittin' it plain.

Left to themselves, trainees would always choose scarves. This involved knitting a long straight piece, with no increasing or decreasing and without rib. It could be knitted very quickly, especially if, into the bargain, trainees managed to negotiate a pattern with broad stripes and few changes of wool. It meant a lot of hand finishing, a long time at a sewing machine and a long wait beforehand until one became free. Scarves had thirty or so tassels and each one had to be done by hand. In this way, by insisting on scarves as opposed to jumpers, girls negotiated social time for themselves (at the heater) away from the machines.

For boys, work was their main motivation. Girls spent most of their time trying to organise their way out of it.

Margaret: They're not interested in learning to knit. Quite frankly, they just don't care.

Supervisors complained continually about the quality of girls' knitting. Girls were not in the business of producing perfectly knitted, perfectly put together garments. Their skills lay somewhere different; in negotiating themselves into positions where they were allowed to knit simple garments in the simplest patterns, to machine-knit them as quickly as possible, then to find ways to spend as long as possible off the machine sitting round chatting to friends. On the machine, garments were knitted anyhow. Backs were knitted with different tensions from fronts. Backs were longer than fronts, then eased to fit at the sewing up stage. Sleeves were too long, necks too loose or too tight. Stitches were dropped, at best, badly picked up, so garments were full of holes. Seams were rarely straight, stripes seldom matched. Girls knitted as quickly and with as little care as they could get away with. They hated ripping work back and correcting mistakes. Often they would hide a piece of work and start again rather than rip something back.

Cath: This is really terrible, Louise. You can do much better than this. Take it back and do it again.

Louise: Ah've ta'en it back three times. Ah'm no' daein' it again.

Cath: Yes you are, come on Louise, back to the machine.

Louise: Nut!

Cath: Come on, I'll start if off for you.

Scenes like this left trainees sulking and unproductive for days. They would sit staring at the same piece of work for ages rather than re-do it.

COLOURS AND STRIPES

Battle lines were drawn around the combinations of colours girls put together in garments. For example, when Joyce knitted her first scarf for herself she was not interested in producing a scarf that she liked; she wanted an easy life. She chose two colours (red and white) and wanted to knit broad evenly-spaced stripes. Broad stripes and two colours of wool meant fewer changes of wool. Cath objected.

Cath: You don't really want a red and white scarf, do you Joyce?

Joyce: Ah dae, honest ah dae. M'brother supports Hearts. It's better than any other gobbin' scarf.

Cath: Look Joyce, the point of knitting a scarf is so you learn to hand feed the wool, you won't learn anything like that.

This time Joyce won and Cath backed down. However, Seafield's scarves typically contained six or seven different colours. For example, two rows of one colour would be followed by six rows of another, four rows, two rows, six rows and so on. And apart from their first scarf, it was only within narrow limits that trainees were allowed any choice. There were continual battles over what was acceptable. Predictably, trainees pushed for the minimum number of stripes and a minimum number of colours. They wanted to use bright colours, where supervisors wanted subtle ones.

Margaret: You need more colours in here. How about adding green?

Jen: Ah hate green. There's enough colours. Ah like it the way it is.

Margaret: Come on Jen, you know fine you need at least four colours.

THE TRANSISTOR

The radio was another area of contestation. Music was of central interest to trainees. They organised their lives around it. In the workshop it was an important talking point and the transistor was important in alleviating the monotony of work. Days on which the transistor was banned were particularly long and boring. This provided supervisors with a mechanism of control. Girls continually struggled to play the transistor increasingly loudly. Supervisors aimed to keep it turned down. Throughout the day, the volume crept ever louder. When a 'good record' came on, someone would turn up the transistor. No-one turned it down again. Eventually a supervisor would complain.

Sue: Turn that thing down, it's driving me nuts.

It would be turned down. Gradually, the volume would become louder again.

Sue: If that thing gets louder again, it's going off for the day.

Eventually it would be banned and trainees would sulk until it was switched on again. Sometimes the transistor was used in a way that was punitive. For example, if girls had been particularly badly behaved and supervisors had lost their head with them, often there was a parting shot:

Cath: And get that transistor *off.*

SMOKING

Smoking was completely banned in the workshop, and girls spent an enormous amount of energy finding space to smoke. They rarely smoked on their own. Indeed, there were frequently two or three girls huddled in a corner, on the balcony, in the toilet, passing one cigarette between them until it was finished. I spent a lot of time in the toilet, chatting and passing round a cigarette. We would stay until our absence was noted and someone came to fetch us.

SORE HEADS AND BAD PERIODS

Headaches, sore stomachs, bad periods were used continually by girls to win time and space for themselves and away from the machines.

Sue: I've handed out ten aspirin in one morning, its a piece of nonsense.

In this context, aspirin took on symbolic meaning. Undoubtedly, girls did get sore heads, but in the atmosphere of the workshop where girls were attempting to get away with as much as possible and supervisors were trying to stop them, everyone was suspect and everyone paid the price. Aspirin were sold to trainees at ten pence each. When trainees complained of bad periods, supervisors, who in any other context would have been sympathetic, were less so in this case.

Cath (to me):

I never know whether to believe them or not. I certainly remember how bad I felt when my period first started.

For trainees, the rewards for being believed were high. It was the ultimate skive. They would either be sent home, or spend the rest of the day sitting at the heater doing nothing, on the odd occasion even being given a cup of tea. Trainees went to and had to go to incredible lengths to prove they were ill. Most were expert. They would spend time in the toilet, pressing in on their stomachs and holding their breaths, returning to the workshop white looking and ill. Someone complained of feeling ill at least once a day.

Linda had looked pale and ill all day. She claimed she had thrown up twice. Cath did not believe her and would not let her go home.

Sue: I think Cath was wrong this time. I followed Linda into the toilet at break. I saw her throw up. She didn't have time to put her fingers down her throat or anything.

When boys skived, it was covert and took the form of carrying-on – horse play, bantering, fighting behind the backs of supervisors. Because the relationship between girls and supervisors was confrontational, skiving was not hidden; it was blatant and it infused every part of their behaviour.

WOOL CUTTING

Sometimes there were hints of more serious disruption. This particular incident happened when I was with joiners. A rumour raged around the workshop that all of the girls had been 'sent home' (suspended). Everyone was curious to find out what had happened. Eighty pounds of wool had been cut through and ruined. People were appalled. It confirmed everyone's worst fear about girls.

Joe: Pure vandalism, it's the worst thing.

The most damning aspect as far as supervisors were concerned was that no one individual girl was responsible. Most of the girls had been involved in one way or another and it was impossible to pin the blame on any one person. Certainly all of the girls knew what had happened and no-one was prepared to give anyone else away.

SUE'S BAG

I witnessed another incident at closer range. It had been a hard day in the workshop. Trainees had been unruly and uncontainable all day. Supervisors were hassled and at the end of their tethers. One confrontation had followed another and Tina was central to most of it. She had been suspended the previous day and had returned to work that morning in a foul temper. She was at her noisiest and least co-operative and had been in trouble all day. The last straw happened in the afternoon when everyone was at their most fraught.

Sue came back in the afternoon to discover that someone had cut half way through the straps of her handbag. All the trainees had known that the bag was an expensive one and a present from her husband. The attack seemed a particularly personal and spiteful one. Supervisors were outraged and determined to get to the bottom of it. The situation looked bad for Tina. It was Sue who had suspended Tina the previous day and Tina had behaved with venom towards Sue all morning. The investigation preoccupied everyone for the rest of the day. First of all Cath collected everyone together in one room. She talked to trainees about the seriousness of the incident and about the importance of finding the culprit. She asked if anyone knew anything about it. A long silence followed and no-one said anything. Cath's last words at that stage were that, if no-one owned up, everyone would be suspended for three days. For trainees, to lose three days' wages was catastrophic.

Her next tactic was to call every girl into the office individually and question her about what had happened. Excitement and resentment ran high. Girls talked and schemed furiously. Despite individual interviews, Cath still found out nothing. She was becoming more and more angry and determined to get to the bottom of it. She called everyone together once more. Again no-one spoke. She told girls that she would leave the room for ten minutes, trainees were to discuss among themselves and decide what to do. If no-one owned up after that everyone would be suspended. Trainees deliberated long and hard, putting every ounce of energy into finding some way round the suspension. When Cath got back they told her they had come to a decision. Netta was the spokesperson. She told Cath that four people knew what had happened. No-one else had any idea. It was suggested to Cath that all four of them be suspended. They were desperately trying to avoid a situation where either one of them was sacked, or all of them were suspended. Cath, determined to get to the bottom of the event, refused to accept this as a solution. Trainees were desperate. A long, glum silence followed and suddenly Pat burst into tears.

> *Pat:* It's no' fair. We're gaunnae get sent hame. Ah ken who did it an' ah ken it wiz an' accident.

At this point Tina too burst into tears. She admitted that it had been her. She was really distraught. She explained that she had been sitting cutting up paper in a temper and Sue's bag was underneath. She said she had been too terrified to admit to it at the time because she was in enough trouble and she knew that no-one would believe her.

Trainees were broken and subdued. Cath had gotten to the bottom of it and had backed down immediately. She said that she recognised and accepted that it had been an accident and no-one would be punished.

YVONNE

Girls were disruptive in many different ways. For example, Yvonne looked younger than any of the other trainees. She wore no make-up and she always looked neat and clean. She wore brown or beige cords and brown jerseys. Yvonne smiled a lot and was unobtrusive. She was painfully shy. Indeed, in all the time I was in the workshop, Yvonne never spoke. If she was asked a direct question, she muttered 'yes' or 'no'. If the question required more than that, she would remain silent, look aside and blush. Supervisors put a lot of effort into making her speak.

Margaret: Yvonne, go and ask Cath what you're to knit next.

Yvonne smiled but did not move. Margaret was exasperated but did not force the issue.

Margaret: You'll have to speak you know. How do you think you'll ever get a job if you won't speak at the interview?

Yvonne's behaviour had implications for her in relation to work. Indeed, viewed as a tactic for gaining space and autonomy in the workshop, Yvonne's tactic was more successful than anybody's. Silently, Yvonne asserted her right to knit only what she wanted to knit. Because of her 'disorder', no-one pushed her to do otherwise. Of all the girls, Yvonne never used patterns. She put together her own combinations of colours and stripes and they were distinctly her own. They were nice to look at but very definitely not in the style of the workshop. After a time they became acceptable, indeed, often copied and ultimately became known as 'Yvonne's colours'. Initially, when Yvonne was told to knit something she did not want to knit, she would knit the garment but knit it anyhow. It would be full of holes, the tension would be wrong and so on. If left to her own devices (which before long she was) and allowed to knit what she wanted, the garment would be perfect. She knitted what she wanted, when she wanted to. For example, one day she had knitted six pairs of socks, all similar. And rather than knit one pair and finish them before going on to the next garment, as the other trainees were obliged to do, she would knit them all one day and finish them the next. Then she would have a spell of knitting only jumpers. She would knit five or six in a week. Some weeks she would knit very little. In this way she quietly built up more autonomy from the boredom and rigours of work than any of the other trainees. The experience of the workshop for her was creative.

Her tactic, though, was double-edged. And, as often happens when women rebel against the structures of their lives, it is in the end often at enormous expense. Jan, the training officer, mentioned Yvonne to me before I even started in the workshop.

Jan: We have one girl here who's obviously very disturbed.

Supervisors too, often mentioned her.

Margaret: She's obviously got a huge psychological disorder.

Cath: Yvonne shouldn't really be here, she should be somewhere where they can help her.

Unlike painters, girls were held in low regard generally. And unlike painters too, inside their workshop they were confrontational. They struggled with supervisors over every aspect of work in an attempt to make space for themselves. In the next section I want to explain girls' attitudes to work, their disruption and their complete rejection of the work that is offered.

GIRLS AND GLAMOUR

I tried to understand boys in terms of their desire for adult status through manual work. If we are to understand the behaviour of girls and what the workshop meant to them, we have to understand their different preoccupations. A concept in understanding girls and their ideas about themselves and work can best be appreciated in terms of 'glamour'. When boys thought of jobs they thought of overalls, tools, 'hooters', 'pieces' and manual work. When girls thought of jobs they thought of 'glamour'.[1] For working-class girls in the early 1980s their expectations in terms of glamorous lives were very low. When they thought about glamorous jobs, jobs way above any expectations about work they might have had, they thought about jobs in offices or in clothes shops, record shops or as hairdressers. Jobs like these existed for girls only in the realms of their imaginations. The most they could hope for were jobs as domestics or cleaners. Girls had realistic expectations of the local labour market and their likely futures relating to it. Their hopes and expectations of glamorous lives were not realised in the workshop, and knitting featured nowhere! The inappropriateness of knitting to girls' lives is I think well illustrated in the following three examples.

SHELL DESIGN

A Community Workshop Project based on knitting was set up in the same premises as the workshop. Elizabeth, the full-time worker, was fiftyish, middle-class and sophisticated. She had experience both of business and of knitting. Her job was to set the project up, find orders, and to be in charge of design and workers. The idea was to employ people external to the workshop as well as ex-trainees. At its peak, it employed eight or so knitters, four or five of whom were 'graduated trainees'. Payment at that time was around thirty-nine pounds. Shell Design felt more like a factory than the workshop. The workforce had fairly rigidly defined tasks – knitters knitted pieces all day long, finishers spent all their time finishing garments off. There was a much more standardised idea of how productive workers should be (i.e. how many pieces should be knitted, finished in one day) than in the workshop. In many ways, the existence of 'Shell' did go some way towards making the girls' workshop more like the boys'. 'Shell' created some real opportunity for the best knitters to move on to something that more resembled real work at the end. Like for painters, there was something to compete for, but the similarity ended there.

Where boys actively wanted to be painters and decorators and grasped

[1]One article which prompted my initial thinking in this direction was 'Girls, Jobs and Glamour' by Norma Sherratt (1983)

any opportunity which gave them a glimpse of it, knitting as a job for girls was a non-starter. Heather was the first of the trainees who was 'sent through' to 'Shell'. Her experience was mixed.

Me: Whit's it like next door?

Heather: Ah quite like it. Some o' the lassies think it's crap an' widnae dae it. It's awffy hard work. Ah'm no kiddin' ye', ah must work three or four times whit ah did in the workshop. The workshop wiz a dawddle compared tae this. An' ye' only git ten pounds mair. It's no really worth it. An' ah fuckin' hate knittin'. Bit it's a job ah suppose.

Other girls were much less compromising.

Louise: Ah'd hate tae be next door. Elizabeth drives ye' like a slave an' a' ye' git is ten pounds mair than here.

On the other hand, supervisors were convinced that the opening of 'Shell' had brought nothing but benefits to girls in the workshop.

Cath: Heather used to be really crazy, a nice lassie, but really wild. She's matured so much since she went through to 'Shell'. She's like a different person.

'Shell' did provide some opportunity to girls which they partly accepted as all that was available. It was a job but an unglamorous one, a poor substitute for what they would like from jobs. Had girls moved on to become trainee hairdressers, or to jobs in offices, the outcome would have been really different. In the case of 'Shell', the offer of a job there was not straightfor-wardly acceptable. Some of them, towards the end of their time, did try to be better-behaved and productive with a view to being sent through to 'Shell'. Most of the girls could take it or leave it, and the opportunity to go through to 'Shell' impinged very little on their attitude to the workshop.

THE OFFICE

Alongside permanent staff in the office, there was also an 'office junior' – a YOP trainee recruited from the ranks of girls in knitwear. For most of the time I was in Seafield this was Linda. Of all the girls in Seafield, Linda was the only one who ever said anything positive about her work. She loved it. The move from knitting to the office had obviously suited her.

Cath: Linda's really freaky looking. She used to be really wild when she was in knitting but she's come on by leaps and bounds since then.

Linda's positive feelings about the job initially puzzled me. Her tasks were minimal, much less than the duties of a 'real' office junior. Linda was never treated as a competent member of the office team. Originally there had been some sort of commitment to teaching the 'junior' to type. Linda rarely touched a typewriter. I was not in the office long enough to gauge what Linda actually did. It was, though, very little. Jobs there were fairly rigidly defined. Jan was in charge of staff training, Alison administered the office in a general way – answering mail, doing wages. Linda hardly participated in these jobs at all. The occasional thing she was allowed to do was passed to her to keep her busy – odd jobs, randomly allocated, such as taking notes to supervisors or adding up a column of figures. She was never allowed to bank money, nor was she even allowed to be in the office alone without the presence of a responsible adult. On my second day ever in the workshop, Alison pulled me aside, told me she had to go to the bank and asked me if I would keep an eye on Linda. I could have been anyone. At that time, Linda had worked in the office for months.

The main function Linda seemed to fulfil in the office was that of looking good. Linda was a fan of Siouxie (of 'Siouxie and the Banshees') and she modelled herself on her appearance. That she had been chosen for the job in the office was no accident. She looked 'punky' but she obviously took a lot of care over her appearance. Her main function seemed to be a reception one. She answered the telephone, received visitors and informed the person they had come to see. Indeed, this was the main reason for the popularity among girls of the job in the office. It seemed glamorous, it was public and provided Linda with the opportunity to build an illusion that it was a real job of the sort that she wanted. Had all the girls been offered similar 'opportunities' the story of their integration might have been a very different one.

THE CANTEEN

The canteen had never functioned successfully. There was another attempt to get it off the ground while I was there. The room was painted, a woman hired. Carol's job was in effect autonomous from the rest of the workshop. Given a float to get started, she paid herself and stocked the canteen out of profits. The hours were short and the pay was minimal. A trainee from knitwear was sent to help her in the subsequent running of the canteen. To my amazement, the choice of trainee was a matter of fierce competition. All of them, it seemed, preferred to be in the canteen than knitting. Fran was the lucky one. The rest of the girls were envious. The canteen was lucrative for a number of reason. In knitwear, the relationship between girls and supervisors felt like that between teachers and pupils. Carol, on the other hand, was and seemed like an employer. As Fran and Carol chatted through their daily chores, the canteen could feel like real work to Fran, work of the type she could reasonably expect.

When the canteen opened, Fran felt fantastic. She dished out food, took money, gave change, cleared tables. She bantered with the boys during their break and also with girls when it was their turn. In this setting, Fran was given one of the few opportunities girls had to feel like they were in real work. In addition, the canteen was also one of the few places where girls could be seen by, relate to and and find out about boys. Fran, though, enjoyed herself too much. After three weeks she was brought to knitwear in disgrace. For Fran it was a public humiliation, a demotion. She was devastated and never forgave the supervisors. She refused to knit anything for weeks.

TO CONCLUDE

Where knitting failed, it was the small peripheral bits of the workshop like the canteen and the office which worked for girls. It was there they found work which coincided with ideas they had about their futures and with which they identified. What girls most wanted and organised their lives around was glamour and glamorous lives. This did not exist for them in knitwear.

For boys, in the absence of real jobs, the workshop offered the next best thing – an atmosphere that felt like work. Girls, on the other hand, hated what they were offered. Where machine-knitted garments can in some circumstances take on an image that is creative and fashionable, to girls it represented something completely different. It symbolised old women, women whose lives were over, women with boring lives stuck at home.

Girls' definitions of the work were utterly at odds with supervisors. Culturally, supervisors and girls were worlds apart.

> *Ruby:* God, if any o' ma pals saw me daein' this, ah'd die. It's whit auld grannies dae.

The work offered symbolised everything they did not want to be.

> *Jen:* Ma da widnae even wear wan o' these.

'Posers' wore stripey jumpers in pubs. Posers were objects of ridicule. Girls felt nothing but distaste for everything they knitted. When they did try on a jumper it was for amusement value only.

> *Netta:* Haw Ally, 'magine walkin' intae a pub like this?

Garments were treated with disrespect. Girls dragged them about the floor by the sleeve, tied them round their heads, round their waists.

> *Joyce:* Ah hate stripes, stripes make me dizzy.

The similar cultural identities of boys and their supervisors in the paintshop meant that boys were well-behaved. In knitwear, supervisors were culturally different from girls, and the craft skills preferred by management were not modified in practice by supervisors with ideas about work that were relevant to girls. Hence, girls felt culturally at odds with supervisors and with work, and the relationship between girls and supervisors was confrontational.

7

GIRLS' ACCEPTANCE OF SEAFIELD

If the last chapter was concerned to outline the reasons for girls' disruptive behaviour, this section discusses the more positive things girls got from it.

APPEARING GLAMOROUS

Girls were preoccupied by the way they looked. With very little else in their lives, the workshop *did* provide them with their major social outlet for appearing glamorous.

Like the boys, girls in Seafield were a fairly ordinary bunch of teenagers with no adherence to one specific cultural style. Their tastes in clothes and music were varied. Linda in the office, for example, dressed entirely in black – black trousers, black twin-set, red lips and orange lips. Her black hair was elaborately styled. In relation to Linda I made my first blunder. Linda had a photograph on her desk in the office.

Me: Is that you?

Linda: Me! Dae ye' think that's me? Naw, it's Siouxie [of 'Siouxie and the Banshees'].

Linda modelled herself on 'Siouxie and the Banshees'. Like Elvis, it was an entirely accepted phenomenon. Everyone called her Siouxie and commented on how good she was at it. Jackie in knitwear was a Debbie Harrie look-alike. She too dressed elaborately.

Not all of the girls looked so exotic. Tina, for example, like all of the girls, was incredibly thin. (Many of them weighed in every day on the wool scales – everybody over seven stones felt awful!) She wore tight jeans and her hair was immaculate, henna'd and sleek. She wore a thin jacket and sandals (without socks) summer and winter. Isobel, Netta, Fran were closest to Tina and they looked similar. There was another group of girls who were friends. They seemed old for their age, worldly-wise and were renowned for being 'laddie daft'. They wore provocative clothes and were generally seen as girls heading for trouble.

The least sophisticated of the trainees were my friends, Yvonne, Louise, Jen, Ruby, Joyce and Pat. Very definitely they were the least successful of the trainees. Their appearance was the least striking. They wore jeans, jumpers and jackets. They would have liked to have looked like Tina but they did not quite make it. They had very little confidence and were quiet and rarely disruptive. Mostly they felt inadequate about themselves, failures in relation to boys and in relation to the rest of the girls. Louise was typical. She dressed plainly because her mother was poor and she had just one change of clothes. She was thin, she chain-smoked and was nervous (her hands shook continuously).

Though different styles were in evidence, what was characteristic of all the girls was the amount of time they put into their appearance. The extent to which girls organised their lives around their appearance was illustrated in the build-up to the workshop dance. It dominated conversation for weeks. The burning issue concerned whether or not to go. There was a general atmosphere of scorn about the event and initially no-one was committing themselves to go. The publicly acknowledged reason was alcohol: there was to be none. Girls felt insulted and upset that the work's dance was to be little more than a party for kids.

> *Louise*: Ur' you gaun'?
>
> *Jen*: Nut! Ur' you?
>
> *Louise:* Ah dunno'. S'fuckin' wild. They're only gaunnae sell us fruit juice.

Alcohol was obviously an important issue, but the real reasons for being doubtful about going were more complicated. Public scorn and coolness belied the strong feelings girls actually had about the event. A general worry was with appearance. Looking good is difficult when you only possess one change of clothes.

Cath was aware of the dilemma about clothes and knew that there was more to their refusing to go than met the eye.

> *Cath* (to me):
>
> It's funny, they're sayin' they're no goin', but they all ordered clothes to wear to it months ago.

Carol (the woman who ran the canteen) ran a 'club' (mail order catalogue) and all the girls were paying up something from their wages. Everyone had ordered something to wear to the disco. Time was running out and as yet nothing had arrived. A lot of the anxiety about the disco and worry about their appearance was displaced on to the late arrival of the clothes. A few days before the party, it was obvious that the order would not come. Girls were, understandably, upset.

> *Tina* (in tears):
>
> Ah cannae go noo. Ah jist couldnae go. The only claes ah huv' ur' the claes ah wear in here. Ah cannae go in the claes ah wear every day.

Tina did go to the disco in the end, but she was miserable. Wearing clothes everyone had seen before was humiliating and spoiled her enjoyment. Seeing so many trainees turn up in their everyday clothes and feeling embarrassed and ashamed about it brought home, to me at any rate, the everyday indignities that go along with being poor, young and working-class in our society.

At the workshop, boys wore work clothes and overalls and tried hard to emulate men at work. Their ideas of how to dress at work coincided with supervisors'. Girls had ideas about appearance and dress which were in sharp contradiction to supervisors'. Schemes were organised around employers' expectations of how young employees should dress. Girls clearly did not dress to meet these needs. They were dressing to meet needs of their own. Consequently they were continually criticised for the way they looked by supervisors. Indeed, the only 'off the job training' they received during the course in a local Further Education college was concerned with this. Yet most of these girls organised their lives both outside and inside the workshop around how they looked. Many of them washed and styled their hair (often elaborately) every morning, often rising at 6.30 a.m. to do it. I certainly found it impressive that, summer or winter, girls could appear at the workshop at 8.15 every morning looking glamorous. In the absence of much of a social life outside the workshop, many of the girls spent their evenings watching television and preparing themselves and their clothes for work next morning. The workshop was (in a sense) their social life and their main outlet for looking glamorous.

NEGATIVE ASPECTS OF HOME LIFE

Another positive feature of Seafield for girls was simply that, in contrast to their often awful home lives, the workshop offered them somewhere else to go. The reality of life for most of the girls outside the workshop was at best boring; at worst, their lives involved circumstances that were depressing and even violent. Having neither the money nor anywhere to go, most of them spent a lot of time at home. In an earlier section, I talked about Tina's home life, and other girls' lives were equally dire.

Marie and Fran

Marie and Fran were 'sisters'. There were eleven children in the family. Their mother was thirty-four. Six of the children were the result of a previous marriage, and she now lived with a man who had five children. Much as they loved their mother, not surprisingly, Marie and Fran were desperate to leave home. They saw their best opportunity to change this through marriage. They had one of the worst 'reputations' in the workshop for being 'laddie daft'. On an everyday level, the workshop offered them both a way out of the house and its responsibilities during the day and the almost only opportunity (however limited) to come into contact with future boyfriends.

Sheila

At sixteen, many of these girls had no family settings at all. Sheila had been thrown out of her house by her father. At sixteen she was homeless. Marie was her friend and she moved in with her temporarily. Marie, Sheila and another of Marie's sisters shared a bed. Marie's mother provided the meals. Later she moved into bed-and-breakfast accommodation with another friend. Sheila had a special interest in me. She knew I had what she wanted – a shared flat. She was continually asking if there were spaces in it, questioning me repeatedly about how many rooms it had, how many people I lived with, how much I paid to live there and where I kept my food. She was worried about sexuality and how I coped with the difficulties of living in a 'mixed' flat. She was well aware that in some circumstances a sixteen-year-old girl is easy prey for men and she wondered how I coped.

> *Sheila*: There're boys in your flat eh? There's boys where we are tae (laughing), we're scared o' them. Dae ye' hae locks oan yer' bedroom doors?

Isobel

Isobel too had no family. She lived by herself in a flat. She used to live in the same flat with her father. At one point in the recent past he moved out and took most of the furniture. Isobel was left there with no-one. Isobel was an incest survivor. The winter I knew Isobel was the coldest for years. She lived in a flat without a bed, without heating and without a cooker. A few months after she came to the workshop, she made friends with Netta. She began to spend a lot of time at Netta's house, sleeping there and eating there, especially at weekends. Undoubtedly the social atmosphere of the workshop, the friends she made there, improved the condition of her life in general. The experience of the workshop was preferable to her life · before.

Louise

Louise lived alone with her mother who was an alcoholic. She had no friends outside the workshop. Most evenings she went home and had some tea, and her mother would go out to the pub. Louise would spend the evening watching television. Her mother would come home from the pub, in Louise's words 'pick a fight' with her and throw her out of the house. Louise walked the streets until her mother sobered up enough to come and find her.

Trish

Trish's home life too had never been easy.

> *Me*: How dae ye' like livin' at hame Trish?
>
> *Trish*: Oct, ah like it fine again, noo ma da's away back tae the navy. Ah like livin' wi' ma ma. Ah hate it when ma da's here, ma ma hates it tae.
>
> *Me*: How's that?
>
> *Trish*: Oct, it's jist that – well we've goat mair money when he's away. He jist drinks a' the time he's hame. An' ma ma gets fat. We eat chips a' the time when he's here. We eat barry 'hings when he's away,

coleslaw an' pasta an' 'hings like that. An' there's lots o' fights. He's ay shouting at her, an' she disnae get oot an' she's miserable when she's stuck in the hoose. Ma ma loves tae get oot. An' a' he diz is sit an' moan.

Me: Where diz yer ma go when she's oot? Diz she go up tae the pub?

Trish: Naw, ma ma disnae drink – she's goat bad healf', she's got a bad heart an' bad nerves. She goes up tae ma grannie's maistly, or up tae ma auntie's. Or sometimes she goes lookin' fur ma wee sister, if she hears she's in toon.

Me: Ye' really like yer ma eh Trish?

Trish: Aye, we get oan barry. Ma ma's ma best pal really, 'specially when ma da's away. She's crazy, she came intae the livin' room last night wi' the dinner in the pot an' she says, 'Come oan Trish, boogey,' an' there we wiz, dancin' a' owr the place. She's really mad, she diz 'hings like that a' the time. When we're up the street she's jist like me, dancin' an' singin'. Only when ma da's away though. She's no' like that when he's here.

Me: How come it's sae different when yer da's away?

Trish: He'll no' let her oot when he's here. He's dead jealous. Ma ma's young an' nice lookin'. An' she's tae sit in the hoose a' day an' night wi' him when he's here. She hates it. An' he's aye goat some'hin' tae complain aboot. He's a' pickin' oan her, 'specially if he's been drinkin'. Or he picks oan me if ah'm late an' she sticks up fur me an' then he fights wi' her. She's oot a' the time when he's away. She's as happy as anythin' when she gets oot. She kin dae whit she likes when he's no' here. An' there's nae arguments.

Apart from her father, Trish's younger sister was an added source of strain in the family.

Me: What diz yer ma dae when she goes oot?

Trish: She maistly goes tae ma grannie's or ma auntie's, or else she looks fur ma wee sister. Ma wee sister's at a school in Stirling. But she keeps runnin' away an' gettin' intae trouble. She went there 'cause ma ma couldnae handle her.

Me: Where's she noo?

Trish: Ma ma heard that she wiz in B.... She always spends a lot of time lookin' fur hur when she's around.

Me: Whit diz she dae in B...? Is she by hursel'?

Trish: Naw. She hings aboot wi' hur pals. She's intae the glue an' she's in wi' a right dopey crowd. Ma ma tries tae find hur afore the police dae. She kens the police beat hur up tae teach hur a lesson.

Me: Where'll she sleep?

Trish: Ma ma heard they were sleepin' in auld railway carriages.

Between her father and her sister, Trish was obviously her mother's main source of support. Like a lot of girls, the workshop offered Trish a place to escape from what would otherwise be the constancy of domestic strain.

The workshop, then, offered girls an escape from what were often difficult home lives. It was for many of them their only social outlet.

Jen: See me, if it wisnae fur ma pals, ah widnae be here at all.

SEAFIELD: A JOB LIKE ANY OTHER

Apart from the social aspect of Seafield, another reason girls kept coming to the workshop was because they had very little expectation that any job would be anything other than boring, irrelevant and without a future, and many saw Seafield like that, as a job like any other, to be put up with and tolerated. Tina was an example. She had three paid jobs (Cath spent a lot of time with her working out her tax). She worked fifty hours a week and for her efforts earned less than forty pounds a week. Her efforts were largely unappreciated in the workshop.

Sue: You don't really care, do you Tina?

Tina: A don't care! Dae ye' ken whit it feels like tae work for £23. 50? Ah'm no' carin' for that!

As far as Tina was concerned, she had three jobs – two cleaning jobs, the job in the workshop, a job like all the others. She worked for money and that largely went to her mother to help her keep house and keep the family together.

Indeed, for many of the trainees their wages represented a lot more than pocket money. In large households often trainees were the only ones with jobs and what they put into the house often represented a significant contribution to the family income. It is very difficult to view the YOP allowance as 'pin money' when week after week mothers would wait outside the gate on a Thursday afternoon to collect 'dig money' from trainees so they could buy food for the family meal that evening.

What the workshop did do for girls was for the first time, probably, provide them with some money that was their own. Until then most had been dependent largely upon poor parents financing them. Their clothes (and controlling their appearance) had often been from mail-order catalogues and 'Provident' cheques. Girls could now, through careful management, have independence to do this for themselves. In the workshop they created, through their own efforts, ways to do this.

One very important characteristic of women's workplaces is the extent to which women pay out of their wages into 'clubs' and 'funds'. Christmas or holiday funds organised on a small scale informally or on a large scale are important features of women's work. For women on low incomes traditionally living from week to week, these clubs are possibly the only way they are able to amass lump sums to finance holidays and Christmas. In the absence of jobs for women it is these hidden things that women also lose. And in Seafield girls too latched on to and created structures such as these and in small ways felt like real workers with real jobs. It was at the girls' instigation that Margaret held money for them in a Christmas Club, and it was Carol in the Canteen who ran the mail-order catalogue – all of the girls were paying every week out of their 'wages' into Carol's 'club' for clothes. Indeed, it was here that the 'realities of trainees' lives' and culture were recognised and that had most relevance to them and went some way towards providing them with an image of themselves as real workers. Unlike boys, who got this sense of identity through what was created by supervisors, for girls, the few opportunities that did exist were unintended, created through their own efforts or by the one working-class woman in the building.

GIRLS' DAILY PREOCCUPATION: ROMANCE

If the content of work in Seafield was seen as irrelevant by girls and they rejected it, what they created for themselves in the workshop in their own time was perhaps their major motivation for being in the workshop at all.

In a previous discussion of boys, I discussed the franticness and desperation the boys felt about their lives and about the way this worked itself out in Seafield. It resulted in the copying of stereotyped ideas of adult male workplaces to the extent of caricature. In terms of gender, this exaggeration implied an exaggeration of abusive and insulting behaviour to women. Girls represented the other side of all this. Where boys were integrated, what girls created for themselves in the workshop was a lot of time and space away from the work to build up and engage in an informal culture of their own. Like boys, girls felt frantic and desperate about their lives too. Clearly though, anxiety was not about jobs (at least not the jobs offered them in Seafield). The central aspect of life for them in the workshop was built around something different.

The overwhelming memory I took from the boys' workshop was of sexism. Their daily references to and treatment of girls as objects to be used and abused, their scathing disregard and contempt for anything feminine, tainted everything that happened there. Boys' culture seemed harsh and brutal in relation to girls, success came in terms of alienated 'scoring' and objectified sex. Girls' culture in the area of personal relationships could not have been more different. Their preoccupations could hardly have been further from ideas about wild sex and scoring. Here, fantasies were romantic. Overwhelmingly, they wanted boyfriends and long-term relationships. They wanted someone to do things with, to hold hands with in the street, someone to take care of them.

Netta: He's comin' up for me the night.

Ruby: he's meetin' me after work tae go roun' the shops. He's gaunnae buy me a jacket.

Fran: Davy's comin' up fur me the night. We're gaun' roun' tae see his big sister, efter.

Jen: He says ah've tae take a day off ma work fur his sister's weddin'. Throwaway remarks like these represented, in fact, the pinnacle of success for girls. Girls referred to boys in a downplayed, low-key way that masked the fact that they were thrilled to be able to make everyday comments like these; actually, very few girls were ever in the position to make them. The comments masked a whole hidden culture of longing and private failure. Remarks like these were often made of boyfriends of two days. They made boyfriends of a few days seem like relationships of long-standing. Desperation was not revealed so much in what girls said but rather in their behaviour.

CREATING THE ILLUSION OF BOYFRIENDS

Where boys' desperation about jobs resulted in their creating the illusion of them in Seafield, girls created illusions as well. Without the existence of real boyfriends, girls made them up. In the absence of anything that could pass for glamorous lives, girls invented them. Many of them lived in elaborate fantasy worlds.

Mary

Mary talked incessantly about Rab:

> Rab's goat the day off work, ah'm meetin' him at break.

> Rab came roon' fur me last night.

> Rab's buyin' me a new pair o' boots fur ma birthday.

The day Mary came in with a diamond engagement ring was her day of glory. Everyone flocked around her, congratulating her and trying on her ring. She was the centre of attraction. Two days later Mary's mother phoned the workshop to say the family were having some trouble with her at home. Mary had created a stir by stealing her sister's engagement ring. Rab was a fabrication.

Mary had had a dismal life. She was unattractive in conventional terms, surly, isolated and unpopular in the workshop. She fought with parents and siblings, lived in an overcrowded house and spent every night in front of the television. She had neither the confidence nor the opportunity to meet and go out with boys. The engagement ring incident was the event which eventually made her leave the workshop.

Louise

I have already described the worst aspects of Louise's life. Louise lived mostly inside her own head. In the absence of any life at all, Louise invented one.

What she invented was interesting and perhaps a bit surprising. Her fantasy boyfriend was no knight in shining armour, coming to sweep her out of her life and into something conventionally glamorous. On the contrary her fantasy relationship was very close to the kind of relationship that she might well one day have, with a few exceptions.

> *Louise*: Ah've finished wi' Rab.

Jen: Whit fur?
Louise: Whit wid you ah done? Ah pours masel' a drink, he pours it doon the sink.
Jen: Ah'd huv' kicked his fuckin' heid in.
Louise: Aye, well. Ah jist tel't him tae fuck off an' no' come back. Then he comes roon' wi' this purple jaiket, right, same as Diane's new yin. Ah fuckin' telt him tae take it back.

Louise invents almost exactly the kind of boyfriend she expects to get. It is not a happy relationship. Nor is it romantic. It has a mundane, everyday feel to it. In it she creates the daily ongoing banter and conflict which she believes to be the stuff of long-term relationships. It is acrimonious and unfriendly, yet (significantly) Louise emerges from every scuffle strong and in control. She fights back, she refuses to take the behaviour he metes out. And because he does not exist, she can send him packing and bring him back any time she wants. Unlike in real life, she can always win.

It could be argued that these stories are extreme. I want to argue that they are not. Louise and Mary were certainly among the most materially deprived of the girls, yet there were other girls, much more deprived, who, because of reasons of style and so on, did make it with boys. There were also girls who had more going for them materially who fantasised even more. All of them spent some time fantasising, fabricating stories and supplementing reality. It is important that Louise and Mary's responses to their lives are not written off and dismissed as pathetic. This kind of behaviour could just as easily be interpreted as a valid response to the very real problems these girls face in creating anything decent for themselves in relation to boys.

I want to move on now to discuss the 'reality' of their relationships with boys. As we shall see, fabricated relationships seem less absurd as the story unfolds.

SPACE TO RELATE TO BOYS

Moving on from my discussion of how girls use the space they create for themselves, I want to look at what they *actively* create. Here I want to focus on two specific examples. These two girls are something of opposites. They capture, I think, the best that was available for these girls and also the worst. First, the worst.

Lena

Netta: Lena's gaun' oot wi' Gavin noo.
Linda: Aw naw! Here we go again. He'll make mincemeat oot o' her.
Netta: Naw, no' Lena. She's as hard as nails.
Linda: She better watch hursel', he's a'ready fancied everybody here.
Netta: Lena's awffy, she'd gaun' oot wi' onybody.

Lena generally wore ripped black tights, a tight black skirt, a white low-cut blouse and copious amounts of make-up. She had dyed blonde hair and

looked ten years older than she actually was. At sixteen she had been
through a lot. Lena had a 'reputation'. She hung about with a group of
about four girls, all of whom had 'reputations'. They were popular and
funny but most of the other girls kept their distance. They were much too
concerned about their own images wholeheartedly to join in.

Fran: See that Lena, she'd dae anythin' absolutely anythin' tae get oot
wi' somebody.

Lena's behaviour was often painfully sad to watch. Her actions seemed to
arise out of desperation. In the few months I was in the workshop, Lena had
been picked up and dropped by almost all the boys. Trish confided in me
one day.

Trish: See, Lena, she's related tae me sortie. She's sortie ma cousin.
She used tae be at the same school as me. Ah couldnae believe it when
ah came here an' seen hur. See at the school, she used tae be barry
lookin'. She'd dead nice hair an' great skin. Hur skin's gobbin' noo.
An' she used tae wear dead nice claes. She's jist a slag noo. Ah widnae
go near hur.

My shift out of knitwear and into the boys' workshop was good news for
Lena. Much to my own (misplaced) irritation, Lena used me to the full.

Trish, myself and several of the boys were sitting downstairs outside the
paintshop waiting for the van and the rest of the boys to come back. Lena
sauntered over. My heart sank. Girls rarely came downstairs. I was her
excuse to make the trip. She strolled past and draped herself around a pole
near me. The ensuing conversation, her mannerisms and gestures were
constructed for the benefit of boys. Her neck was covered in 'love bites'.

Lena: Are tha' marks still oan ma neck, Anne?

Me: (reluctantly):

Aye

Lena: That wiz some pairty last night. It went oan till three in the
mornin'. Then me an' these three guys drove through tae G.... It was
barry

I bagged off wi' Phil at Joyce's party last night.

Me: Phil? I thought you wir efter Steve?

Lena: So ah wiz, bit, Steve couldnae make up his mind, so ah jist
bagged off wi' Phil.

At work next morning, when Lena went down to see Phil, he completely
ignored her.

Netta: Lena's hud the K.B. [knock back] fae Phil.

Louise: Dinnae take it Lena. Dinnae let him get away wi' it. Go up an'
say some'hin' tae him.

Lena: Oct, ah'm no' that bothered.

(much later)

Ah'm stayin' away fae them noo [boys]. Ah never want tae see
another one.

Lena: (later still):
Netta, whit's Smarties' phone number? Gaunnae ring him up fur me?

Lena wanted a boyfriend. But she used dangerous and potentially disastrous tactics to get it. And the way she was behaving now would certainly have implications for the rest of her life. With every new attempt to create what she wanted, the possibility of ever getting it became more remote. Already she was stuck with an image of herself and a 'reputation' she did not want. And the more obvious it became to Lena that she was not going to get a steady boyfriend, the more desperate she felt and the more compromising became her behaviour. She hated herself and could see no way out of her predicament. And behind her funny, jokey and flighty manner, lurked nightmares with which she was forced to live.

Lena: Anne, huv' ye' ever wanted tae be deed?
Me: Naw, no' really.
Lena: Ah huv'. Ah wish a' the time ah wiz deed. Ah wish ah wiz back at school.

Lena would disappear out of the workshop in the morning, leaving the rest of us to cover up. She would arrive back gleeful at lunchtime.

Lena: Ah'm gaun' oot wi' Colin noo. We're gaun' roun' the shops at break.

Elation would last only until next morning when, of course, she would be dropped.

Trish

Trish: Who is it up there fancies Elvis?
Lena: Dunno'.
Trish: Who wrote 'ah think Billy's [Elvis] smashin' oan the bog wa'? Did you see it Anne?
Me: Nut!
Lena: Sheena wiz gaun' oot wi' Elvis till last week.
Trish: Aye, ah ken, but it's finished noo.
Me: (really surprised):
Wiz she? How dae you ken that? Ah didnae ken that.
Lena: God Anne, yer slow oan the uptake.

Trish and Lena could not have been more different. Lena would undoubtedly end up in the worst of all possible worlds. In fact, Trish wanted a boyfriend every bit as much as Lena. What Trish had learned, though, was to go about it in an altogether different and more shrewd way. In her own setting, Trish was cool, confident and sure of herself. This was unusual. She had a reputation for being fussy and careful about who she went out with. At sixteen she had had numerous boyfriends, but she did not have a 'reputation'. Her standards were relatively high. In the workshop she worked slowly in relation to boys, hanging back, sussing out who was who before she risked making a move.

Like the rest of the girls, by far the most important and time-consuming work that Trish did was social relations work. She knew all the painters by name after two days (long before I did). She quizzed me continually about what I knew about girls (having already spent two weeks there). She learned which of the boys had money and who had none. Trish's mother gave her a packet of cigarettes every day, and Trish always passed cigarettes to boys who had no money to buy them for themselves. She knew which of the boys had run out of money to buy lunch or who was strung out on glue and fed them food.

Trish: You want a Kit Kat Frankie?

Ah've goat a piece oan cheese if ye' want it Mo.

Trish was as interested in getting a boyfriend as Lena was. But unlike Lena, she carefully built up an image of the kind of person she wanted to be, of how she wanted to appear in the workshop. She thought about what she wanted, developed a strategy and acted accordingly. She covered up her real interest behind a detached, but caring and sisterly façade. She had learned early and somewhere else to be cool, to hide her feelings and to play games in relation to boys. She earned the reputation of being hard-to-get and fussy. Boys responded to these tactics and were interested in her. Yet the tragedy of Trish's story is that for all of this the outcome for her was only marginally better than for Lena.

THE SAGA OF TRISH AND ELVIS

Trish: Ah'm gaun' oot wi' somebody noo.
Me: Yer' whit! Whit are ye' oan aboot. Ye' wirnae gaun' oot wi' anybody yesterday.
Trish: Aye, ah ken, but ah am noo. Ah'm no' kiddin' ye'. Min' ah wiz tellin' ye' that Andy [Fiona's boyfriend] had a pal ah fancied. Well, Fiona telt Andy an' brung him roon' tae the hose last night. Ah'm gaun' oot wi' him noo.
Me (laughing):
God, ah cannae believe this.
Trish: (laughing): Aye, but, there's a wee bit o' a problem. Ah'm no' sure if ah like him noo.
Me: Whit! Ye' started gaun' oot wi' him last night an' yer finishin' wi' him a'ready.
Trish: Oct, it's no' that. He's a barry guy an' that, an' we get oan barry. Bit, it's jist that, well, there might be somebody else.

And once again I had been slow on the uptake. Eventually Trish dropped enough hints for me to work out what had been going on. Trish fancied Elvis (hence all the interest Trish had shown earlier in her conversation about Elvis with Lena). And it was at this stage, in relation to boys, that Trish lost her cool. Disappointingly (for me), when Trish decided she wanted a boyfriend, she also wanted it badly enough to risk a lot, to play the same degrading and humiliating games as everyone else. Her obsession with Elvis dominated (and altered) our relationship for weeks. And once again (as Trish's closest friend in the workshop) I had an important role to play. Trish used conversations with me to pass information to Elvis, and I was a substitute for communicating with him directly. Infuriatingly, everything Trish said to me within earshot of Elvis was designed for him to hear.

Trish (loudly):

Ah'd like tae take ma jumper off, but ah've goat oan a see-through tee shirt an' ah dinnae wear a bra'. Well ah sometimes wear black yins – that's the only colour ah wear.

Anne, whit am ah gaunnae dae? Ah've goat this huge problem. Whit wid you dae? Ah'm nearly gaun' oot wi' wan guy, but ah really fancy somebody else?

Relations in the workshop were such that before long all of the trainees knew what was going on. It was public knowledge that Trish fancied Elvis. And before long all the girls had a role to play. First of all the network of girls (with Trish's approval) transmitted to Elvis that Trish was interested. He could not believe his luck and responded quickly. He began hanging about where she was, making contact with her and directing comments to her. The rest of the boys were quick off the mark as well and began directing their own helpful comments at Elvis.

Mo: Stop moonin' aboot Elvis, yer' makin' a complete arse o' yersel'.
Gibber: Look at Elvis, he's in love.

A side of Trish I had not yet seen emerged. In front of Elvis, she was submissive, coy, giggly and shy. We discussed her dilemma endlessly.

Trish: Anne, ah'm gaun' mad. Whit'll ah dae? Ah cannae jist tell him [the first boyfriend, Gerry] ah dinnae want tae go oot wi' him. He kens fine it wiz me wanted tae go oot wi' him in the first place. He'd think ah wiz aff ma heid. An' anyway, he kens where ah stay, he'd jist come up. Whit'll ah dae?
Me: Ask Elvis oot.
Trish: Ask him oot! Me! Ye' must be jokin'.
Me: Well, two-time Gerry.
Trish: Na, ah widnae dae that. Naebody's ever done that tae me. Well Mikey did, once, bit he wisnae good-lookin' enough tae get lassies. Ah went oot wi' loads o' guys jist tae get him back.

In the workshop things reached fever pitch. Trish and Elvis increasingly directed looks only at each other. Cigarettes, as ever, played an important role socially. Elvis cadged 'fags' from Trish. Trish bantered about how Elvis was always on the cadge. Matches passed continually back and forth. They joked about work.

Elvis: Ye' call that sanded? Ye've missed bits a' owr the place.
Trish (blushing):
It's better sanded than anythin' you ever dae.

Elvis: That bit's no' even touched. Tam'll make ye' dae it again.

Trish: Shut up. Ye' dinnae even ken whit yer talkin' aboot.

Meanwhile, Trish was becoming increasingly tongue-tied and embarrassed when he was around. Sometimes, as he passed, he would take the brush out of her hand and do a bit of her work merely to assert his authority.

There were several implications for Trish in her involvement with Elvis. Firstly, it greatly increased her standing and confidence among girls. They were impressed. And personally I lost a lot of power in my relationship with her. Initially, because Trish and I had been thrown together, the only two girls in a male workshop, being older gave me an advantage. I was slightly more able to cope with the general embarrassment of being in the workshop than she was. But increasingly, as it became obvious that boys were interested in her and not me, her status in relation to me rose. For example, Trish and I were inseparable at lunchtime. One breaktime, during the time when Trish and Elvis were at their most undecided, I felt utterly worn down by the bantering. I suggested to Trish that we sit on the balcony in the sun to eat our 'piece' (rather than sit with the boys as usual). A new Trish asserted that she was staying inside. I sat outside by myself sulking. She laughed and played cards inside. At teabreak, Trish, the boys and I played cards inside.

Trish's success with boys and my lack of it continually defined and redefined our relationship. It allowed her to become increasingly assertive and independent in relation to me and in relation to the rest of the girls. But of course what Trish gained in relation to me and the rest of the girls, she paid for highly in relation to boys. To get Elvis meant behaving in ways that were compromising and in ways which threatened her whole future in the workshop. Her behaviour with Elvis meant forfeiting being seen as equal to and treated as a sister by the boys. She was no longer one of them. For the first time she gave boys an opening to see her as silly and coy and like the rest of the girls. Overnight she became an object to be appraised, put down and ridiculed. Her every move, everything she wore, was remarked upon and commented on.

My main anxiety about Trish in this situation was that her job was in jeopardy. She was risking the only role that was possible for her in the workshop. As someone who was flighty, interested in boys and treated by them as available and pursuable, her credibility in the eyes of the staff would diminish. The saga of Trish and Elvis dragged on.

Trish: Ah finished wi' Gerry last night.

Me Whit happened?

Trish: Dunno'. Ah jist telt Fiona tae tell him no' tae come back up fur me.

Me: 'Cause o' Elvis?

Trish: Aye. Ah'm funny like that. An cannae get intae one guy when ah fancy somebody else.

Me: D'ye think ye'd still be gaun' oot wi' Gerry if ye' didnae fancy

Elvis?

Trish: Aye, likely.

Trish was quiet and unhappy all day. She had finished with one boy to make space for another. Elvis had still not made a move. The other girls again came to the rescue.

Sheena: Hi, ah went an' asked Elvis if he fancied you.

Trish: Did ye'? Whit did he say?

Sheena: He admitted it.

I expected Trish to be upset and angry at Sheena interfering. On the contrary, she was pleased.

Trish: (to Sheena):
If ye' see him, tell him ah fancy him an' a'.

This was a significant step forward: a public admission of mutual interest.

Several days later, Elvis had still not taken the initiative. Trish was frantic. Previously she had been certain that she would never ask anyone out. In the face of such inertia from Elvis, her resolve faded. She spent a day agonising about it.

Trish: Think ah should ask him oot? D'ye' think ah should? Wid you dae it? Should ah dae it at break? Dae ye' think he'll think ah'm a slag? Dae ye' think he'd dae it if ah jist left him?

That day something was bound to happen. Everyone knew it. People grinned expectantly at one another all day. I felt nervous. I was well aware of the potential repercussions for Trish. Firstly, it would provide Elvis with information about Trish to pass on to the rest of the boys and, secondly, regardless of how Trish behaved, she would be labelled, discussed and her life as a serious painter in the workshop would be precarious.

By four o'clock Elvis and Trish had got as far as throwing screwed-up pieces of paper at each other. I knew the inevitable would happen as they clocked out and walked together to the bus. The next scene is best left as an excerpt from my fieldnotes.

> I usually walk to the top of the road with Trish, but I was so pissed off at her and Elvis mucking around in the cloakroom, I was so anxious and nervous for Trish, that I left first and walked up the road by myself. I knew they were behind me. I knew she was going to ask him out. I could almost hear her asking him through her giggles. I felt sick to the pit of my stomach. When I sneaked a look, my last image was of Elvis picking her up in his arms like a baby and subjecting her to a long passionate kiss. Elvis, with his slicked back hair, his black leather jacket, had maintained his Presley image to the last. The last group of boys walking behind were cheering. It was as much as I could do to disappear round the corner as quickly as possible.

The story did not end here. On Monday morning I arrived early at the workshop, anxious to find out how Trish's weekend had gone. Trish was in a state again.

Trish: Ah'm supposed tae be gaun' oot wi' him noo. He thinks ah am.

But ah'm no' wantin' tae. Oct, ah dunno' whit's wrong wi' me. He's a barry guy an' that. We jist went back tae ma hoose oan Friday an' ma ma gave us fish fingers an' chips. Bit, ah'm really stupit – ah jist dinnae feel like gaun' oot wi' him noo. Ah dinnae ken whit's wrong wi' me, ah jist go oot wi' a guy once an' then ah'm no' wantin' tae any mair.

Trish offered many layers of explanation herself. From afar, Elvis seemed more attractive than Gerry. Close up there was not much to choose between them. And Trish had not been impressed by Elvis's behaviour after work on Friday.

> *Trish*: Did ye' see him? Did ye' see whit he did? He picked me up, right in front o' a' tha' guys! Ah could've killed him.

Trish completely avoided Elvis after this, giving him no opportunity to pursue her. The romantic flush was over, the reality of having a boyfriend in the workshop dawned on her. She knew boys would talk about and discuss her. Less besotted with Elvis, it was all of a sudden clear to her that to survive in the workshop, to maintain her strength and credibility, she had to be sexually neutral.

Much later, when the incident had blown over, Trish offered a more considered analysis of events.

> *Trish*: Ah went oot wi' Elvis fur wan night, an' ah finished wi' him the next. A' the lassies thought ah couldnae get him tae go oot wi' me. Ah ken't he wid. Ah jist hud tae prove ah could dae it. An' when ah knew ah could, ah didnae want him ony mair. Ah'm dead funny, ah'm jist like that.

Two weeks later, Trish was engaged to Gerry. Gerry was unemployed.

SPACE TO DISCUSS BOYS

I want to move now to a consideration of girls' sexual politics in general. For working-class girls, especially when (as then) the material circumstances of their lives were deteriorating, problems were extreme. All of these girls displayed at different times insights into their lives that were both perceptive and, for me, humbling. Few of them were under any illusions about the state of the world and their role in it.

> *Netta*: Could you ever be a stripper Anne?
>
> *Me*: Naw, ah don't think ah could ever dae that.
>
> *Netta*: Ah could, sometimes ah could really imagine it. Ah could never be a prostitute but.
>
> *Me*: Oct, sometimes ah'm no' that sure that it wid be any different tae whit a lot o' women pit up wi' fae their men onyway. Ah bet a lot o' men force their wives tae huv' sex wi' them a' the time.
>
> *Netta*: Aye, ah ken. Must be horrible that. (To Pete who is listening) Think you'd ever force yer' wife tae huv' sex wi' ye' if she didnae want tae? Bet ye' wid! Maist men wid!

They had very few illusions about sex. At sixteen many of them had been through numerous sexual relationships and encounters with boys and men, and few of these experiences had been positive. Jen had already had an abortion and had very strong views on the subject.

Jen: When we were at school, right, we used tae go along an' barney wi' the folk that believed in God. One day we wiz talkin' aboot abortion an' this posh lassie wiz comin' oot wi' so much pish – aboot God bein' in a' life an' so we couldnae kill it. Ah could've killed her. Whit diz she ken aboot haein' bairns ye' dinnae want. Ah telt her ah'd raither hae a million abortions afore ah' hae wan wean ah couldnae look after.

They knew about and felt angry about the 'double standards'.

Ally: (passing on advice to me):
They kin sleep wi' a thousand burds. You sleep wi' wan an' yer' a slag.
Louise: Guys ur' dead selfish. Whit ah hate is that ye' kin never be sure whit they're askin' ye' oor fur. Ah 'ate it. Even if they seem really interested in ye' an' ye' go oot wi' them fur ages, it kin still turn oot that they've only been efter wan thing – an' then they're off. It makes me really mad.

Girls here did not, however, passively accept the double standard. They continually devise ways round it. And the strength and ingenuity with which they manage to carve maximum space for themselves from minimum and diminishing resources was indeed impressive. Trish found her own way round the dilemma. She told me one day she was on the pill.

Me: Dae ye' no' feel under a lot of pressure tae huv' sex wi' guys if they ken yer' oan the pill?
Trish: (smirking):
Naw, no' really. Ah dinnae tell them!

In this way Trish could be seen to be both pure and experienced at the same time: an old double standard, a newish way round it. She could give boys enough (in their terms) to keep them interested but be protected and appear innocent at the same time.

Frankie: Ah 'hink every burd in Great Britain should be oan the pill. That'd be magic.
Trish: Aye, magic fur yoos. It'd be much worse fur us. Everybody expects ye' tae sleep wi' them as it is. It'd be horrible.

Later Trish and I continued on the conversation on our own.

Trish: Ah've goat a funny attitude tae sex. Ah need tae be gaun' oot wi' a guy fur ages afore ah huv' sex wi' him.
Me: Dae ye' ever feel ye' should be huvin' sex jist cause yer' oan the pill?
Trish: Aye, it makes ye' feel like that – ah dinnae though. Some o' ma pals dae. They'd sleep wi' absolutely anybody jist 'cause they're oan the pill. This lassie ah ken, she sleeps wi' everybody – men an' a'. She's a real slag. There's this guy in oor street, he's aboot fifty. He

kind o' helps young folk. A' ma pals hing aboot his hoose. Abbe goat chucked oot the hoose by hur da' cause she wisnae comin' hame an' she moved in wi' him. Noo, she's sleepin' wi' him an' everything. When I was off sick one day, my pals in Margaret's room filled me in on the conversation I had missed.

Jen: Aye, ye' missed yersel' yesterday. We wiz talkin' about sex – or she wiz [pointing to Louise] – ah dinnae talk durty.

Louise: Don' gies it. You're the worst o' the lot.

Jen: (laughing):
Yer' a fuckin' liar!

Me: Right, come oan, whit'd ah miss?

Louise: Nuthin', we wiz talkin' aboot nuthin'.

Me: Ye's wur', whit wiz it?

Pat: We wiz talkin' aboot sex.

Jen: Aye, an' she wiz sayin' plenty.

Pat: Louise says she hates it 'cause it's sair. Ah hate it tae. It hurts ye' sae much.

Louise: Ah hate it when guys go up ye'. Ah think it's horrible.

Jen: (laughing):
Ah widnae ken, ah dinnae let him near me.

Louise: Yer' a fuckin' wee liar.

Jen: Ah am nut.

Louise: Guys are fuckin' thick anyway, they dinnae huv' a fuckin' clue.

THE POLITICS OF THE DANCE FLOOR

I want to look at the girls' sexuality in wider terms still, and how boys and girls in the workshop came together in the formal setting of the 'works dance'. The disco took place when I was in the girls' workshop. In most of what I say here, girls are central. I would like to have had a fuller understanding of how boys experienced the party, but it is impossible to be in two places at once.

I have already talked about girls' anxiety in relation to clothes in the build-up to the party. Scorn was poured on the idea. The publicly-acknowledged reason was alcohol. There was to be none. People felt insulted, upset that their 'works dance' was to be nothing more than a party for kids.

Louise: Ur' you gaun'?

Jen: Nut! Ur' you?

Louise: Ah dunno'. S'fuckin' wild. They're only sellin' us fruit juice.

Real reasons for not going were, of course, more complex. Public scorn and coolness for the event belied the strong feelings that were actually around. Once again it took me a long time to understand that underneath, girls were anxious. Anxieties existed on all sorts of levels and not simply around what to wear. Publicly, Jen was as scathing as anyone.

Jen: Fuckin' sure ah'm no' gaun' tae a crap 'hing like that. That's weans 'hings.

Privately, to Louise and me, she revealed that her anger had a different root.

> *Jen:* Ah walked oot o' his hoose last night. Ah'm seek.
>
> *Me:* Whit happened?
>
> *Jen:* Oct, it's him. Ah asked him tae go tae the pairty wi' me an' he widnae. An' he says he'll finish wi' me if ah go masel'. Ah'm seek.

As the date crept closer and more and more people were deciding to go, Jen became more and more miserable.

A lot of anxiety was simply because girls were scared. They were afraid that the cool façade they projected in the workshop would be difficult to maintain in a setting where they were expected to relate to boys directly. They were nervous about appearing young and naïve in front of their pals, afraid of boys themselves (they might not get a dance or be able to talk to boys without making a fool of themselves). All these things meant that the idea of the disco loomed large for weeks and real fears became displaced on to superficial discussions about the presence or absence of alcohol.

BEST PALS AND DANCE FLOOR CULTURE

I use the event of the disco to explore the importance at this time in their lives of girls' relationships with each other and to illustrate the importance of the workshop in affording them the opportunity to create this. (The phenomenon of 'best pals' is also mentioned by Angela McRobbie 1978).

The life of working-class girls without 'best pals' has probably always been limited. Without a close pal, there would be no-one to spend time with, to shop or to play records at home with. There would be no one with whom to discuss boys, hair and clothes. Above all, without a best pal, girls would have limited access to public space. Girls relied on each other for a social life. Without each other, going to a disco, or simply for a drink, would have been impossible.

> *Me:* Whit dae ye' dae at night?
>
> *Trish:* Mind Fiona? She left here jist efter you started. She's ma best pal, ma only pal. She lives roon' the corner. We wiz born in G… then when we moved tae P… Fiona moved tae. I go doon' there every night fur an hour between six and seven. That's the only time ah see her noo 'cause Steve [Fiona's boyfriend] goes tae see her every night at seven. Ah used tae spend every night roon' there. Fiona's great. See me an' Fiona, we can say anythin' tae each other, absolutely anythin'.

I arrived at the party with my friends from Margaret's room, Louise, Ruby and Fran. Fran had conveniently picked up Phil the day before. She had the dubious honour of being one of the few girls to be there with a boyfriend. Netta had come with Carine (her best friend from outside the workshop) and Louise and I made a natural twosome. Had I not been there, Louise would have been miserable. We stuck together like glue. The group sat round one table.

The boys hung about in groups on the other side of the hall. We all came together on the dance floor. The contrast between 'on the floor' mixed-sex culture and 'off the floor' culture when girls were by themselves was remarkable. 'Off the floor', girls were relaxed and funny. Banter and insults flew. 'On the floor' everything tensed up. Girls assumed different personae, walked stiffly, danced without communicating. They were cool, detached and 'laid back'.

To Ruby's irritation, one guy homed in on her friend Carine from the beginning. The incident built up without words. Every other dance, he would saunter over and dance opposite Carine. Ruby would immediately sit down and sit out the dance. Carine would dance one dance, silent and aloof, then she would sit down. Back in her seat, unobserved, Carine's veneer would crack. She would slump, giggle and blush. Sitting on Ruby's knee, she would avidly discuss him and her chances of 'bagging off' with him. Cool and composed once more, she and Ruby sauntered on to the dancefloor. The guy came over once more and Ruby sat down. Two dances this time. On the second dance he moved across. Carine and he kissed passionately for ten minutes. Everyone returned to their seats. Carine was obviously flattered. She was pleased with herself for playing the game well. However, this time her luck was out. The guy did not follow events through to their logical conclusion. He decided instead to pick up someone completely different on the last dance. Disappointed (but putting a brave face on it), Carine (and Ruby) left for the last bus.

At a couple of points during the evening, when Carine was tied up and Ruby and Louise were dancing, I left my small circle of friends to play Good Samaritan elsewhere. Everyone it seemed (including staff) had managed to get round the 'no drinks' ban and were high on glue or drink. The consequences of treating adolescents as sub-adult (for their own protection) and not allowing drink pushed them into finding their own solutions to the limitations imposed. It had the opposite to the desired effect!

Netta and Isobel were also best friends. They related to me with glee the story of how they had arrived at the disco. They had bought a bottle of vodka on the way. They also bought a bottle of 'Irn Bru'. They replaced half of the Irn Bru with the vodka.

> *Netta*: God, ye' should huv' seen us oan the bus Anne. Isobel kep' turning' tae me an' sayin', 'Netty, would-you-like-a-small-sip-of-this-lovely-Irn-Bru'?

Both were incredibly drunk, Netta no less than Isobel. Isobel spent the first half of the evening slumped in a chair with her head in her hands and the second half curled up under the sink in the toilet. Isobel was out of action for the evening. Had I not been there, this would have been a social disaster for Netta. Once again I made myself indispensable.

> *Netta*: Come oan Anne dance.

Anne, ye' gunnae chum me tae the bog tae see Isobel.

Ye' gaunnae chum me tae ask the boy at the disco tae play the
Eurythmics.

If you do not come in twos you do not dance, and if you do not dance you
do not get boyfriends.

THE OTHER SIDE OF BEST FRIENDS

These were the supportive and positive aspects of female relationships, the
sensitivity and awareness teenage girls showed towards each other. Angela
McRobbie noted this too, that girls' own private culture 'is characterised by
a tremendous sense of solidarity between the girls and in particular
between "best friends"' (McRobbie 1978: 106). The close emotional attach-
ments, the informality of relationships between girls of this age were and
are real, and in many ways more satisfying than anything that could be
achieved with boys. Boys and girls seem to be brought up to want different
things from relationships with each other. Boys want to 'score', girls want
stable relationships. What girls seem to be able to have with boys is loaded
with cultural expectations. Ideas about their futures are bound to fall short
of the casual easy friendships girls can have with one another.

But like Angela McRobbie, I also noticed that friendships between girls
were double-edged, that they were marred somewhat by alternative
motives (McRobbie 1978). Girls interpreted their relationships and
friendships in the light of taken-for-granted ideas about their own future.
Friendships with each other were temporary, something to be appreciated
on one level as a stop-gap, as a means of achieving the boyfriends and
husbands they were so powerfully made to want and to need. McRobbie
noted that the driving force behind female friends was the desire to work
together to get boyfriends (1978: 106). No matter how important a friendship,
the unspoken assumption behind it is always that it would take second
place to the possibility of getting boyfriends. Fiona and Trish in this study
were incredibly close, but it was always understood in their relationship
that it took second place to Fiona and Steve.

> *Trish:* Ah used tae see a lot mair o' Fiona. But noo she goes back tae
> her ain hoose at seven o'clock tae see Steve.

Trish regretted this state of affairs but understood it.

When I danced with Netta at the disco, when a guy came over to her I
automatically left the floor to sit down. Netta gave me a meaningful look
over her shoulder. It was sympathetic, but the shrug said quite clearly, 'Too
bad, the world's like this.' I still felt rejected and undermined as I walked
away. And close as Carine and Ruby were, when Carine danced with her
boy, Ruby did everything in her power to facilitate Carine getting off with
him. She discussed tactics with Carine and provided entertainment on the
way home to cheer her up. Both went home to Ruby's house and drank tea.
They talked and laughed until the early hours and both ended up in Ruby's
bed.

TO CONCLUDE

In their own autonomous setting, girls were strong and articulate. In how they related to boys, girls were utterly different. The following incident provides an illustration of this.

The task of the day was cleaning the carpet in the workshop. A chance to get out of knitting, this was a sought-after job. Without boys, it was a noisy, colourful affair. Ridiculously dressed in nylon overalls, woolly hats pulled down over their eyes, socks and gloves to keep out the dirt, and armed with huge sticks for beating carpets, They lugged the cumbersome carpet over to the garden to be beaten. Spirits were high. they jumped around hugging each other, laughing, sweating and giggling. Grunts of exhaustion were interspersed with curses and screams. Wit, abuse and insults flew.

> *Heather*: Fuckin' help, right, Ah'm no' standin' aboot here while you gawk at Colin.
> *Joyce*: Wait, ma hat, ma hat, it's fell owr ma eyes. Wait, wait, ma stick's broke.
> *Heather*: Yer' spots are much better the day Netta.
> *Netta*: Aye, ah ken. Ah jist discovered that crisps huv' goat oil in them. They're bad fur yer' spots. Ah'm gaunnae eat fruit at break fae noo oan.

After beating the carpet.

> *Heather*: S'awffy bad fur yer' spots, dust. Ah'm gaunnae go an' scrub ma face.

The arrival of two boys utterly transformed the scene. Two painters, attracted by the noise, appeared at the top of the garden. Their presence and then their approach created havoc.

> *Heather*: Christ, the laddies are comin'.
> *Netta* (snatching off her woolly hat):
> Whit am ah like, whit am ah like? Whit like's ma hair?
> *Joyce*: Fuck, ah've goat spots an' ah look hellish wi' ma hair back.

Embarrassment increased as the boys approached. They took the sticks from the hands of the girls as their right and took over beating. The girls were crushingly embarrassed about the way they were dressed. Reduced to an awkward silence, they sat away from the action, backs turned, unable to speak. To the boys, they appeared cowed, weak and silly. When the boys left, the transformation was equally dramatic.

> *Netta*: Whit dae ye' 'hink o' Colin? [Colin had just finished showing his prowess as the best carpet beater]
> *Ally*: Total arse hole.
> *Netta*: Ah quite like him.
> *Ally*: He's goat a new wee moustache comin' in an' he 'hinks he's *it*. He's only been here fur three weeks an' a'ready he's fancied everybody.

With boys around, girls' behaviour altered drastically. What they said,

how they said things, changed. Mannerisms were tight, nervous and coy.
When boys discussed personal relationships, they talked about 'scoring' and about sex.

Pete: That burd wi' the skinheid an' the nae teeth would go out wi' onybody.

Frankie: Ah'm no' kiddin' ye' man ah could've gaun' oot wi' any wan o' tha' burds at Snowie's pairty.

When girls discussed it, it was to create the impression that they were in long-term relationships (often when they were not):

Fran: He disnae like ma hair like this.

Pat: He says he's gaunnae buy me a jaiket fur ma birthday. Ah dinnae even need yin.

Boyfriends of a few days took on the aura of forty-year-old marriages.

Fran had picked up Phil the day before the disco. In relation to the rest of the girls, her standing rose enormously. From the moment she asked him out, she discussed him in the most familiar of terms. It was as though he had always been her boyfriend. Again, somewhat surprisingly, it was not the romantic element in her relationship that she played up. She played that down and gave the impression of matter-of-factness. She familiarised him by never referring to him by his name, rather 'he' or 'him'. Far from being romantic when she was with him at the disco, far from being in a mood of showing off her new boyfriend, Fran was matter-of-fact. More than anything, she wanted to convey an image of long-termness and possessiveness. She flicked dust from his collar, held his jacket, searched the pockets of his jacket for cigarettes as her right. They spent most of the evening bickering, about him leaving her too long by herself, about the girls he was eyeing in her presence. It created the illusion not of a new relationship, but of a marriage of long-standing.

Fran: He's meetin' me efter work, we're gaun' fur a walk.

In their separate workshops, then, where boys were integrated and contained in trying to appear like real workers, girls were irrepressible. They rejected the discipline of Seafield and were strong and clever in their resistance to authority. But for girls, freedom was paid for at a price. And the franticness that girls felt about their lives was transferred, not on to a desperation about jobs but, all too predictably, on to feelings of desperation about boys, boyfriends and relationships. And so many of the positive things that girls created for themselves in Seafield, the way they effectively made space for themselves and alleviated boredom, how they generated their own informal activities, the autonomous culture they so carefully and successfully build up, was ultimately organised around boys, boyfriends, engagements and husbands.

In the absence of real jobs and anything reasonable which could substitute, girls, undaunted in their search for glamour, increasingly defined themselves out of the job market altogether and looked for it from relationships with boys and marriage. In Seafield, for girls, a preoccupation with jobs took a back seat. The desperation they felt about their futures, their search for glamorous lives was displaced, deflected and mediated on to obsessions about their ability and inability to get and to keep boys. The whole of their autonomous culture was organised around creating effective space and time to find out about and to be with boys. Thus, space and time they won for themselves was used ultimately to manoeuvre into situations where they could find things out about boys (sewing socks on the balcony, for example, exchanging information in the toilet). When girls got together off the machines, it was generally to talk about boys. All of their energy went into gathering and piecing together information about boys. (This was certainly one of girls' best, if most misplaced, skills.) And facts were amassed and gathered in the most adverse of circumstances – from odd chance meetings on stairs, from boys themselves as they engaged in the more boring aspects of their jobs, sweeping the balcony outside the knitwear workshop. Girls would shout direct questions at boys over the balcony either for their own interest or for one of their friends. They would observe boys from a distance, or rely on family and friendship networks outside the workshop to fill in gaps about boys' personal biographies. In this way girls knew a lot about boys. They knew their names; where they lived, who their friends were, who they went out with. This activity was not reciprocated by boys. Often it took boys a year to find out the names of the other boys, far less know the names or anything else about girls.

It is easy to make light of this – talking about boys is what teenage girls always do and have always done. But this obsession with boys had very serious implications. And it did not happen here simply because teenage girls are 'like that'. Here it was the result of the very real material circumstances of their lives which left them with very few choices. And witnessing some of the strongest and most assertive young women I knew behave in degrading, submissive and frantic ways in the hope of improving their lives through men, was not something to be taken lightly.

Far from being irresponsible, irrational, happy-go-lucky teenagers, by the age of sixteen these girls already carried huge burdens of responsibility. Many had already faced poverty and homelessness, joblessness and difficult relationships. Many had already played a vital and pivotal role within their families, holding parents together, mediating (often physically) between them, caring for younger members of the family, cooking and cleaning. The reality of sex for many working-class teenagers was (and is) far from romantic (making nonsense of such sentiments as 'puppy love'). The material reality of the lives of these teenage girls, their dependence on parents, their lack of freedom and lack of money, the fact that parents expected them to be asexual, meant that when sex did occur it was often hidden and less than desirable. And where the pill and the sexual 'freedom' of the sixties is now being discussed in critical terms, for these young women, the effect of this era have been perhaps even more of a mixed blessing. Sex was often the result of a physical struggle. Summer or winter, physical and sexual encounters happened outside: in shop doorways, at bus stops, derelict buildings, garage lockups. It was in a car if you were lucky, outside in the countryside or at parties. There was always an element of haste. It was often cold and someone could interrupt. Girls were picked up, beaten up and expected to have sex. And what passed for sex happened in the least conducive of circumstances. It was often brutal, with someone you did not really want and it usually ended in a physical struggle. The early sexual experiences of most working-class teenage girls tended to be not only humiliating and painful, but dangerous as well. Often it amounted to little more than rape. Many of the girls in the workshop were sexually experienced and most of them had been pushed every inch of the way.

8

CONCLUSION

I have focused here not on the more spectacular sub-cultural responses of working-class young people, but rather on the relationship of ordinary Scottish teenagers to the new institutional arrangements designed to deal with the problems of their unemployment. In doing this I have tried to understand the different arrangements for and the responses of both girls and boys.

In the paintshop I outlined the way in which an adherence to the world of (manual) work created an environment which reinforced gender stereotypes. It excluded girls rather than moved any way towards offering them alternatives. I outlined the struggle of one particular girl to be accepted. To do so, she had to be seen to be sexually neutral and non-threatening.

For boys in the paintshop, I argued that working-class ex-tradesmen there were able to create an environment and flavour of work which allowed boys to build up and reinforce images of themselves which they had of being real workers with real jobs. This was what they desperately wanted and they were largely well-behaved. Disruption, when it occurred, was not confrontational or threatening to the running of the workshop. In the absence of real jobs, at least for boys, schemes which most replicated work gave them most confidence.

In joinery, because supervisors were reluctant to impose on boys a harsh regime and were more lenient, they were less able to create an atmosphere through which boys could create the illusion of real work. This workshop was less relevant to boys who were less accepting and more disruptive.

I would suggest that in a situation like this where the material circumstances of their lives were deteriorating, aspects of masculinity, for example, the need to feel like real men with real jobs, were heightened. There was also little evidence to suggest that ideas generally held about women as objects of sex to be used and abused were altered for the better. On the contrary, boys never discussed girls in anything other than the most disparaging of terms.

Unlike painters, girls in knitwear were held in low regard. Also unlike painters, inside their workshop girls were confrontational. They struggled with supervisors over every aspect of work - over what to knit, what colours of wool to use, over how to put patterns together. Supervisors tried to make girls knit complex garments; girls tried to knit the simplest. They struggled to spend as little time as possible on their machines. Girls rejected work. This was partly explained in that, unlike boys' supervisors, in knitwear supervisors were unable to create work which was culturally relevant for girls or provide them with any image of themselves that they wanted. Rather, teaching skills which were essentially craft skills meant the atmosphere felt more like a school needlework class than work. Girls' cultural identities were less about work than about the pursuit of romance and glamorous lives. Knitting in no way fitted this image of themselves. They rejected it.

In so far as Seafield was acceptable to girls, it was for reasons other than work. They were able to build up an autonomous culture of their own and this was important. In the absence of money or opportunities to indulge in leisure outside the workshop, the workshop provided girls with the social opportunities to appear in the world as glamorous. They spent evenings at home preparing for work, spent days creating the space to fantasise about, to find out about and relate to boys. In relation to authority in the workshop, girls were as enterprising and assertive as any of the 'lads' in Paul Willis's study. What was different was that girls here built the space they so cleverly created for themselves around boys. And ultimately it locked them not into a lifetime of manual work (like Willis's 'lads') but into something worse – a lifetime of domesticity and dependence on men.

YOP TO YTS

As my study was coming to an end, YOP was being replaced by YTS. As already mentioned, YTS (unlike YOP) was not a short-term measure introduced to deal with the numbers of unemployed young people; it became the mechanism for delivering training and managing the transition from school to work for all 16 and 17-year-olds. However, in Seafield, the transition from YOP to YTS in the workshop did not change very much. Had it changed and taken on the criticism of YOP, it might have jeopardised the whole basis upon which the success of the Seafield was built – and it very nearly did.

As Seafield moved to fulfil the new conditions of YTS, there was a push to streamline the workshop. A new manager was appointed whose ideals were more in line with the new vocational ideals of the MSC. Where the old manager had allowed Tam to create the feel and atmosphere of a real workplace, Frank (the new man) wanted supervisors to be more like teachers, boys like students. He tried to introduce formal lessons in numeracy and literacy and was more interested in effecting a change in attitudes than in providing trainees with trade skills. Without understanding the basis of boys' acceptance of the workshop, he tried to change it.

Whether or not this would have worked with trainees or not is open to speculation. In the first instance, the changes met with resistance from supervisors.

> *Tam:* Ah've been a tradesman a' ma life. Ah've been dealin' wi' apprentices for God knows how many years, an' he thinks he can come an' tell me whit tae dae wi' ma laddies. Ah've been here longer than anybody. It'll be owr' ma dead body.

Frank's strategy met with similar results in the joinery shop. Here, too, the enthusiasm for broadening boys' minds and providing them with a more creative alternative to the harshness of real work was directly in opposition to Joe. Frank saw the important work that Joe did was 'benchwork'; he wanted to expand that. Joe had other ideas.

> *Joe:* Rockin' horses an' jigsaw puzzles! Can ye' see these laddies? These laddies should be raisin' frames an' hingin' doors and batterin' in nails, no' makin' bloody rockin' horses.

The paintshop was relevant to boys because of who supervisors were, what was on offer and the way in which it was offered. Frank did in the end understand the difficulties of involving himself too much in the day-to-day running of the workshop and he withdrew. Seafield continued like this almost unchanged as a YTS Mode B scheme.

IMPLICATIONS FOR FUTURE SCHEMES FOR YOUNG PEOPLE

I do not intend to spell out in a detailed way the implications for change which result from the experience in this particular workshop. For one thing, this is not straightforward. For example, from an appreciation of the culture and background of the girls, it is easy to understand their attitude towards knitting. It would be another easy step to allow girls to knit what they wanted. To do this would undoubtedly make the substance of girls' everyday existence at Seafield more meaningful. At the same time, the knitting workshop raised questions about introducing such a traditional women's skill into their training, and a skill which would have little place in the local labour market. There are also questions which could be asked about mixed workshops, where boys and girls would have access to all the skills. The advantages and disadvantages of this are complex. A mixed workshop would have fundamental implications for the organisation of the workshop and for its success and relevance to staff and trainees.

It is also important not to lose sight of some of the positive (if perhaps unintended) consequences of the scheme. For example, we saw how the early sexual experiences of girls were far from ideal. This has undoubtedly been true for generations of working-class girls. Here, however, these new institutional arrangements meant, if nothing else, that girls' first relationships were more likely to take place in a sheltered context. Before the development of such schemes, girls were dropped into an adult world at sixteen, taking such vulnerabilities as we have seen here into the world of work. At the very least, in the workshop, girls' early sexual experiences (bad as they were) tended to be with boys of their own age and not with adult men.

More generally, I would argue that for any future developments in youth training, staff training had to be a key consideration. And by staff training, I do not simply mean 'trainer training'. If equal opportunities is to be taken seriously there needs to be training here too. I would also argue that any improvement also requires that those involved in service provision receive training in and have access to information about teenagers and about youth culture.

With regard to equal opportunities, I would argue that attempts to break down gender stereotypes by the MSC are important. Introducing a note of caution, I would also argue that too much should not be expected from such attempts. Because of the very nature of schemes like these, attempts inevitably only scratch the surface. There are a number of reasons for this. First, while schemes exist to give young people a taste of the world of work and while gender stereotypes remain unchallenged in the world of work, nothing much will change. Also, this age group is in the process of forming gender identities which are fragile. What they most want is an adult identity and adult status. The world of work holds the promise of this, gender relations and all. At this point in their lives, asking them to reject and challenge traditional roles and relations of work is perhaps asking too much. It may be more important simply that they are given training which is relevant to them and which may afford them a point of entry into the world of work. If nothing else, this chapter re-emphasises the importance of women's financial independence.

For a number of reasons, it is important to understand and respect youth culture. Cohen (1984: 126) has outlined assumptions on which YOP and YTS were based. Young people were 'ignorant of their rights and weakly motivated to defend them. They lack any kind of work experience. They have no access to useful information and advice other than that provided by official and professional experts. They have difficulty in organising their lives in a rational or satisfactory way.' This assessment belies the fact that when it came to the local job market, both boys and girls had a good knowledge of it. They were sometimes better informed about what was possible for them and had better means to achieve it than could be offered by the local careers service. As already mentioned, far from being irresponsible, by the age of sixteen many of the trainees, particularly the girls, already carried huge burdens of responsibility. I agree with Dan Finn when he says about young people: 'Essentially they are not really in need of many of the social and life skills on offer from the MSC and its training programmes – of 'coping', 'resisting provocation', 'taking orders', 'getting on with fellow workers' and so on – because they have already had so many of these experiences and learned how to cope with them competently and realistically' (Finn 1984: 54). They were already familiar with such things! For anything to change in the future means taking into account and respecting their culture. It means taking into account the different cultural needs of girls and boys. It means bearing in mind the conditions of the local labour market and building something on the basis of that.

The young people in this study passed through YOP a decade ago. Yet despite the transition to YTS and despite the social and demographic changes of the 1980s and 1990s, the process which still mediates the shift from school to work for tens of thousands of young people remains remarkably unchanged, not least with regard to understandings about young people, their skills, their needs and their culture.

THE WIDER CONTEXT OF TEENAGE LIFE

In this chapter I looked at how boys and girls worked out the new conditions of their lives in relation to the workshop. It must also be borne in mind that the changes described here developed hand in hand with much wider changes in their lives. Taken together, these meant a declining standard of living and affected every aspect of their lives. It also meant a declining of material standards for their families.

Since then the recent Social Security changes have effectively left 16 and 17-year-olds with no independent status at all. For those not on YTS it leaves most of them with no entitlement to benefit. For those on YTS it leaves them still without the financial means to support themselves outside of their families. An increasing number are 'cut off from an anticipated future of leaving home, material consumption and marriage. In place of… a traditional passage to adulthood there is now a period of extended dependence on the state and on a sometimes unwilling family' (Finn 1988). Poverty and declining material standards must be the worst position of all from which to build good-quality youth training.

BIBLIOGRAPHY

Ainley, P. and Corney, M. (1990) *Training for the Future*, London: Cassell

Allen, S. *et al.* (eds.) (1985) *The Experience of Unemployment*, London: Macmillan

Bates, I. *et al.* (1984) *Schooling for the Dole?*, London: Macmillan

Brown, A. (1990) *The Context of Change: The Scottish Economy and Public Policy*, in Brown and Fairley (eds.) (1990)

Brown, A. and Fairley, J. (eds.) (1990) *The Manpower Services Commission in Scotland*, Edinburgh: Edinburgh University Press

Brown, S. (ed.) (1988) *Education in Transition*, Edinburgh: SCRE

Cockburn, C. (1983) *Brothers: Male Dominance and Technological Change*, London: Pluto

Cockburn, C. (1987) *Two Track Training: Sex Inequalities and the YTS*, London: Macmillan

Cohen, A. K. (1955) *Delinquent Boys: the Culture of the Gang*, Chicago: Free Press

Cohen, P. (1984) *Against the New Vocationalism*, in Bates *et al.* (1984)

Cole, M. and Skelton, R. (eds.) (1980) *Blind Alley*, Heskith; Ormskirk

Fairley, J. (1990) *An Overview of the Development and Growth of the MSC in Scotland*, in Brown and Fairley (eds.) (1990)

Fiddy, R. (ed.) (1983) *In Place of Work: Policy and Provision for the Young Unemployed*, Brighton: Falmer Press

Finn, D. (1984) *Leaving School and Growing Up: Work Experience in the Juvenile Labour Market*, in Bates *et al.* (1984)

Finn, D. (1987) *Training Without Jobs: New Deals and Broken Promises*, London: Macmillan

Finn, D. (1988) 'Why train school leavers?' in *Unemployment Bulletin* (Autumn) Unemployment Unit: Trojan Press

Frith, S. (1980) *Education, Training and the Labour Process*, in Cole and Skelton (1980)

Furlong, A. (1988) 'But they don't want to work, do they?' in Raffe (1988b)

Goldstein, N. (1984) 'The New Training Initiative: a great leap backward' in *Capital and Class*, No. 23

Griffin, C. (1985) *Typical Girls: Young Women from School to the Job Market*, London: Routledge and Kegan Paul

Hall, S. and Jefferson, T. (eds.) (1975) *Resistance Through Rituals: Youth Subcultures in Post-War Britain*, London: Hutchinson

Heidensohn, F. (1985) *Women and Crime*, London: Macmillan

Lees, S. (1986) *Losing Out*, London: Hutchinson

Loney, M. (1983) *The Youth Opportunities Programme: Requiem and Rebirth*, in Fiddy (1983)

Markall, G. (1982) *The Job Creation Project: Some Reflections on its Passing*, in Rees and Atkinson (1982)

Markall, G. and Gregory, D. (1982) 'Who cares? The MSC interventions: full of Easter promise', in Rees and Atkinson (1982)

McCrone, D. (1984) *The Scottish Government Yearbook*, University of Edinburgh

McRobbie, A. (1978) 'Working class girls and the culture of femininity' in Women's Study Group (1978)

McRobbie, A. and Garber, J. (1975) 'Girls and subcultures', in Hall and Jefferson (1975)

McRobbie, A. and Nava, M., (eds.) (1984) *Gender and Generation*, London: Macmillan

MSC (1977) *Young People and Work: Report on the Feasibility of a New Programme of Opportunities for Young People* (Holland Report)

Mungham, G. (1976) 'Youth in pursuit of itself', in Mungham and Pearson (1976)

Mungham, G. (1982) *Workless Youth as a Moral Panic*, in Rees and Atkinson (1982)

Mungham, G. and Pearson, G. (1976) *Working Class Youth Cultures*, London: Routledge and Kegan Paul

Raffe, D. (ed.) (1984) 'Youth unemployment and the MSC. 1977–83', in McCrone (ed.) (1984)

Raffe, D. (1985a) *Youth Unemployment in the UK. 1979–1984*, paper commissioned by the International Labour Office

Raffe, D. (1985b) 'Change and continuity in the youth labour market: a critical review of structural explanations of youth unemployment', in Allen *et al*.(1985)

Raffe, D. (1988a) 'Going with the grain: youth training in transition', in Brown (ed.) (1988)

Raffe, D. (ed.) (1988b) *Education and the Youth Labour Market*, Falmer: Lewes

Rees, T. and Atkinson, P. (1982) *Youth Unemployment and State Intervention*, London: Routledge and Kegan Paul

Roberts, B. (1975) 'Naturalistic research into subcultures and deviance: an account of a sociological tendency', in Hall and Jefferson (1975)

Sherratt, N. (1983) 'Girls, jobs and glamour', *Feminist Review* No. 15

Whyte, W. F. (1955) *Street Corner Society*, Chicago: University of Chicago Press

Willis, P. (1977) *Learning to Labour: How Working Class Kids Get Working Class Jobs*, Farnborough: Saxon House

Women's Studies Group (1978) *Women Take Issue*, London: Hutchinson